The Inverted **Gaze**

Arsenal Pulp Press | Vancouver

The Inverted **Gaze**

*Queering the French Literary Classics
in America*

François Cusset

Translated by David Homel

Originally published as *Queer Critics*
Copyright © 2002 by Presses Universitaires de France.

THE INVERTED GAZE
by François Cusset
Translation copyright © 2011 by David Homel
Preface copyright © 2011 by François Cusset

ARSENAL PULP PRESS
#101–211 East Georgia Street
Vancouver, BC V6A 1Z6
Canada *arsenalpulp.com*

Liberté · Égalité · Fraternité
RÉPUBLIQUE FRANÇAISE

This book has been supported by the French Ministry of Foreign and European Affairs, as part of the translation grant program. Cet ouvrage est soutenu au titre des programmes d'aide à la publication du Ministère des Affaires Etrangères et Européennes.

This book was published with the support of the French Ministry of Culture—National Center of the Book. Ouvrage publié avec le concours du Ministère français chargé de la culture—Centre national du livre.

The publisher gratefully acknowledges the support of the Government of Canada (through the Canada Book Fund) and the Government of British Columbia (through the Book Publishing Tax Credit Program) for its publishing activities.

Design by Shyla Seller
Editing by Brian Lam and Robert Ballantyne
Cover photo by Henry Horenstein, The Image Bank

Printed and bound in Canada

Library and Archives Canada Cataloguing in Publication:
Cusset, François
    The inverted gaze : queering the French literary classics in America
/ François Cusset.

Translation of: Queer critics.
Includes bibliographical references and index.
Issued also in an electronic format.
ISBN 978-1-55152-410-8

    1. French literature--History and criticism. 2. Homosexuality and literature. 3. Homosexuality and literature--France. I. Title.

PQ145.1.H66C8713 2011   840.9'353   C2011-905385-3

CONTENTS

A Queer World

We live in a queer world. Or such is the term an old-style British aristocrat would use when referring to our strange world: odd, dodgy, mysteriously disjunctive, charmingly dysfunctional, often tragically wrong. A world in which the only available choice for queer people seems to be between globalized forces of the lowest common denominator and the various reactive bastions of gregarious pride. In other words, a choice between the lonesome figure of the commodified individual and the warming effect of group therapy—or else, between the masturbatory shame of consumer society and the submissive sex orgies of identity politics. However you name them, though, such opposing forces are far from incompatible. They might even altogether form an alliance that excludes from the scene any sort of alternative, as witnessed by the examples of multicultural marketing, diversity as a gimmick used by human resources, and the happy marriage today between Islam and neoliberalism from Dubaï to Istanbul. Great news: the twenty-four-hour shopping mall and the fetish of cultural identities are finally engaged; wedding details to be announced. What makes things more confusing in France, a country of the past, with its shrinking power and its legacy of nostalgia, is how the very icon brandished as the only safeguard against both identity politics and globalized market forces—i.e., the just and magic "Republic" with its abstract principles and wishful universalism—sometimes appears as nothing more than one other type of identitarian bastion (the French one), and at the same time as a trick used by France's sales reps to promote what the country has to sell to the outside world: classical culture, the lyricism of history, luxury goods, and mass tourism. By staging themselves as the heroic enemies of both the market's nihilism and identitarian dead ends, the defenders of the good ol' humanistic "French Republic" reveal who they are in the larger global context, perhaps unwillingly, as if they had been tricked by themselves: the French are but one exotic tribe with its specific folklore and stylish arrogance, and one distinguished commodity highly priced on the global market of abstract values and historical legacies.

All right. Now, why re-tell this queer tale of French vanity, a known paradox offering nothing new under the sun? Well, because it is the exact impression I had, less than a decade ago, in view of the polemical initial reception of this book (entitled *Queer Critics*) in France: apart from utter indifference, which is always the dominant reaction to *any* book (especially to books on alternative re-readings of literary classics), I was left with a moralistic critique on the one hand and an identitarian one on the other, uncomfortably situated between two types of rejection: between the explicit wariness of France's abstract universalists who saw "queer theory" as a typically American product of the 1980s Culture Wars, and the even more direct disgust expressed more or less openly by the French gay scene's "official" intellectuals and reviewers. The former viewed that little pink book—since it was the cover shade chosen by my very academic French publisher, Presses Universitaires de France—as a dangerous attempt by American multiculturalism and gay studies to penetrate the French fortress of universalism and the nation-state, while the latter saw it as an ironic and typically heterosexual (who said I was?) game with academia's gay politics and queer science, guilty of not taking seriously what was indeed so serious, or guilty of its very ambivalence. And here one should never forget that ambivalence has been France's definition of the devil ever since World War II and the traumatic experience of its collaboration with the Nazis: between clear-cut Hitlerites and a handful of early resistance fighters, the rest of the country was then like a "swamp of ambivalence" (*le marais des ambivalents*), a silent majority all too cowardly to make a choice and too sly to tell the(ir) truth. So here I was: one more ambivalent trickster, an ambivalent passenger who hadn't clearly handed his identification papers over when crossing the border. I was a traitor to my nation according to the old-style, anti-American proponents of abstract universalism, as if I had sold my soul to cultural studies and identity politics. And in the opposite view, that of the self-appointed parish of Gay France and Parisian queer thinkers, I was a traitor to the gay and lesbian cause and to the future of queer theory in France (where it had never been heard of before, my book being the first one with the word "queer" in its title to have been written in the language of Proust and Balzac), my own playful approach denounced by them as a typically heterocentrist mockery—when in fact I had intended it, on the contrary, to be a very queer exercise.

This small story of the small initial reception to my small book wouldn't be worth telling if it was not the symptom of much larger, and saddening, tendencies, both in 2002 as well as today: the tendency of queer experts to believe they own that very field and hold a copyright on that very term, criticizing outsiders for daring to set foot on their turf; the tendency of a declining (but still powerful) French elite to cling to their flawed principles and outdated certitudes almost hysterically, as if the dream of a better humankind was to die with them; and last but not least, the tendency of objective enemies (since the ideologues of anti-identitarian French republicanism and the activists of France's gay community should indeed be enemies, or at least structurally opposed) to hate the very same books and, one might add, to sign a peace agreement and symbolically reconcile over the same scapegoats. Back in 2002 I was such a scapegoat. And god knows why, I like this idea.

10   The notion I have put to work in this book (according to which it might be interesting to extend the work of literary critics along their own lines, and even push their own interpretative audacities deliberately further, or *too* far) raises a serious question of methodology and indeed contradicts many dogmas of academic integrity and intellectual rigor: as such it is arguable, if not perilous, but I have done it for the sake of intellectual experimentation, naïvely thinking that it was more interesting to experiment with literary criticism, at the risk of bad faith and contradictions, than to maintain it on its institutional tracks, at the risk of boredom and conformism. Again, I might be wrong about that, and I am ready to take full responsibility for it, but nothing could make me happier in this context than to have the opportunity to let English-speaking readers judge for themselves. As for the other danger—that of opening fortress France to a byproduct of American culturalism and identitarianism—this critique, already absurd back then, has of course been proved entirely wrong ever since: in less than ten years, intellectual and academic France has finally opened up to these very issues of identity politics, minority readings, and cultural struggles, which are now discussed everywhere else in the world. France has even started to catch up on neighboring countries for the translation and dissemination of the best of recent American theory. While belated, this trend is crucial, at least if France wants to remain active in international debates, and one which my modest pink book, without knowing it, indeed inaugurated: queering stiff and elegant France as the first move toward a critical reawakening French-style, and toward letting France rejoin (finally) the global politics of critical theory. It might not have been the right time then, but it is high time now—such things in fact can change in less than a decade. Thus born from a very French situation—and born from and against a queerless or anti-queer French atmosphere—this book nevertheless does have things to tell the more familiar readers of *11* queer theory in North America. In that sense it is back where it departed from, after a very queer French diversion.

One last word: I can only praise the magnificent work of translator David Homel, who produced in English a text undoubtedly better than the original French (if such is the very queer paradox of translation) and who patiently followed me on the path of far-fetched puns and re-phrasings, making all of them miraculously accessible in English—for this and for his enlightening and friendly attitude all along, I want to thank him warmly. But as he and I had discussed early on, there is one pun which he couldn't translate, an easily forgettable one for sure were it not for the explicit autobiographical dimension it adds to a text (and a larger preoccupation) that is itself queer enough to never use the first person explicitly: in calling "q.c." the various North-American queer interpreters of French literary classics, I was not only coining an acronym for "queer critics," I was also attempting to join the group, sneaking myself onto that list, insofar as in spoken French the two letters "q.c." sound exactly like my last name. That said, I might have invented a new function for prefaces such as the one you are reading: helping an author come out of whatever closet he was in, especially when he hadn't dared to do so in the text of his book itself. But forget about me; welcome to the forbidden museum of French literature, with perhaps a few surprises to be discovered under the dust. Self-oblivion, and the dusting off of a few sex toys: if that is not queer, nothing is.

I also extend my gratitude to my editor at Arsenal Pulp Press, Robert Ballantyne, whose energy and availability are what any author can dream of, as well as to my two original editors in France, Paul Audi and Roland Jaccard, series editors for "Perspectives Critiques" at Presses Universitaires de France, for their support in this adventure and their uncompromising intellectual independence.

—Berlin, March 2011

Everything that shatters something, everything that 13
breaks with established order, has something to do with
homosexuality, becoming animal, becoming woman,
etc. All breaking of semiotic codes implies a breaking of
sexualization. In my opinion, it is not worthwhile asking
oneself about homosexual writers, but instead, we are
better off seeking what is homosexual in any great writer,
even if he is a heterosexual.

—FÉLIX GUATTARI

INTRODUCTION

Holes in Glory

> What do queers want? [...] not just sex.
> —MICHAEL WARNER, *Fear of a Queer Planet*

Glorious abysses. In certain specialized locations, the term "glory holes," a classic of the American queer lexicon, refers to those openings cut into the sides of stalls, through which may appear the surprise of an anonymous member, hanging softly or in triumphant erection unless, while waiting for a partner in turpitude, these holes are more like a bull's-eye, an opening through which, alone with his desire, someone's arrival can be glimpsed, noisily unbuckling his belt and pressing his belly against the entry, then thrusting an anonymous turgescence into the fray. Abysmal glory. Through such glory holes that indeed poke holes, according to them, through every important text, a handful of American critics have proposed, over the last twenty years, a new expression of literary history, in order to spy upon, like voyeurs, somnolent bodies of work, to bring new outrage to untouched classics by mixing in their own libido—to tease a reaction from literary works that have been studied too piously and that, glimpsed suddenly through the interstices, might reveal an entire secret postulation of self-love. The narrowness of the hole, the length of what may traverse it, the heft of that which, still unclear, might appear from the other side when nothing obstructs it: these are the principles of a new geometry. In the insistent gaze of this distanced eye, as an enterprising hand slips through the opening for a caress, a new disturbance shakes the canonical texts, be they symbolist sonnets or Gothic novels, epic poems or historical sagas, a quiver on the surface of the sentences that will quickly multiply our monosemic reading and finally unveil, beneath the hetero plot and the accepted forms, a darker layer from which the impulse to write will spring—an immemorial layer already present in all writing long before a Prussian neurologist imposed, around the year 1870, the modern definition of homosexuality.

From New York literary cafés to California campuses, these experts in abyss, "perverse" readers as they call themselves, are more or less thrown together—despite their distrust of all categories—into the new classification of "queer critics" (that we'll call QCs for convenience's sake). Just as pejorative as "fag" or "fairy," the term "queer," taken from familiar speech and used by homos among themselves (stealing from homophobes the privilege of the insult, the way blacks sometimes call one another "nigger," depriving racists of a similar pleasure), by its very register appeals to a more slippery status, much less formal, than the label "gay," currently in use. Contrary to the assigning of identity assumed by the word "gay," "queer" enjoys the uncertainty of play, in the sense of provocation and the enlarging of a field. "Queer studies," when applied to literature, sees itself as a way of questioning in a more transgressive manner, especially when compared to the circumscribed approach characteristic of "gay studies." Whereas the latter seeks to establish a homo counter-corpus, as canonic in the end as the official corpus (and traveling parallel through literary history from Shakespeare to Oscar Wilde, from Virginia Woolf to Proust), the former does not limit its field of investigation to any pre-established criteria, explicit thematic, or author biography, preferring not the celebration of difference, but rather the insinuation of constant doubt, and the political, playful, and insatiable erosion of the usual borders between homo and hetero. Just as we would all be a little bit that way, all literary texts are too, those arising from the English and American traditions of course—queer critics love to play on North American campuses—as well as those from each national literature: Germanic, Hispanic, and French.

The queer approach is less frequently applied to the major texts of the French corpus compared to those of the Anglo-Saxon, but still widespread enough, judging by the large number of essays and articles published in the field of French studies over the last while, so we can now establish a counter-reading of the august French tradition. Inverts and sodomites, onanists and transsexuals, androgynes and hesitators now emerge, in studies offered by queer critics, between the lines of the apparently most innocent of all classic works of French literature. Tempting fissures appear in the façades of our academies, and swell the volumes of dusty surveys of world literature with forbidden pleasures. In France, the famous couple of French literature schoolbook editors, Lagarde and Michard—two rear-guard soothing homophobes read by many a French schoolchild—are now being deflowered by American critics, the latter teasing out the truth about the collaboration of those two mustachioed Frenchmen. Nothing's more exciting to sully than noble manners, or more enjoyable to corrupt than the *esprit* of the serious man. Among all national literatures, French remains the most fiercely defended, the only one that dares present itself as an autonomous whole, to lay claim to Orphic chosenness. So then, to lead it into delinquency, according to queer logic, is as pleasurable as blasphemy, as tempting as a swift kick to good manners.

In a word, nothing is more gratifying than to stuff the oh-so-

French properness of our men of letters down their throats, and to profane, with a questioning raised finger, the shadowy graves of our Greats. But let's not forget that when it comes to unzipping our dusty literary corsets, American readers are not the only skilled practitioners. They don't have the monopoly either over homo-reading or hermeneutic jubilation. If British or Brazilian critics have teased out our cherished corpus, very French readers have also initiated us into the pleasures of the twisted gaze: Serge Doubrovsky turned Don Juan into a prudish old lady and Sartre into a coprophagic demiurge, Michel Butor pounced upon Montaigne's slips, and Yves Citton hunted down impotency and inversion in the work of Crébillon and Stendhal. In this context, what's noteworthy about American readings is that they have come to form a school, and that by centering their attention on French texts (far from the practitioners' complacency called up by these French writers), they deploy the set ritual of an object relation. A true act of reading that intends, according to the case at hand, to be a violation of simple homoerotic playfulness.

This book is not just out to review the interpretations of certain French classics by certain American critics, a monotonous parade of university extravagances unknown beyond their borders. Our objective is much freer: we want to try out their game, learn under their guidance how to "un-read" the classics, lightening the American arsenal of its heavy theoretical load—that often turns similar analyses into pontificating treatises of sexual epistemology—better to deploy the entire reading experience, the reader's pleasure and caress. Even if it means at times pushing the envelope of their suggestive meandering, blurring the border that separates the fair review of these readings from their personal extensions, even if it means hijacking the hijackers, turning them inside out, paying them paradoxical homage that the ironic slippage of reading pleasure will provide. But before approaching the "glory holes" of the French corpus, we first need to select the texts, both the literary sources and their queer commentaries, and sort through the array of exposed bodies – a far less scholarly sorting, livelier and more urgent, similar to plumbing the depths.

To that end, we will follow the curves and projections of chronology, the familiar bestiary of a partition by century with its distant vignettes, Middle Ages orgies, Renaissance Socratisms, minor slip-ups of the Grand Siècle and the shadows behind the Enlightenment, the Industrial Revolution's bourgeois inverts, and, for the twentieth century, the androgynous spasms of an imploding novel, a sort of Greco-Turk survey of a pathway set down by Roman numerals. This, less out of the need for historical conformity than by the imitation of the queer gesture, since they are numerous in North America: those who justify the division by century, pointing to the evidence itself, in case it escaped you, that when it comes to literary matters, "History—and not just family history—is an erogenous zone."[1] But once we've duly respected this scheme, whom do we choose among the profusion of ambiguities that haunt our literary history? The list is endless, unfolding from the pages of collections of queer critics: Villon, Montaigne, Rousseau, Voltaire, Diderot, Sade, Balzac, Baudelaire, Gautier, Rimbaud, Verlaine, Mallarmé, Zola, Maupassant, Proust, Gide, Colette, Cocteau, Jouhandeau, Green, Sartre, Genet, Yourcenar, Maurice Sachs, and of course Violette Leduc. The list of characters is just as lengthy, from Orgon to the Mother Superior, Vautrin to Michel Ménalque, from Albertine to Querelle, from Inès Serrano to all those poor Hadriens. In the QC way of seeing things, additions are always welcome, supplemental uncertainty for a catalog that does not seek its own end. Go ahead, have a look at what is least

---

1 Louise Fradenburg and Carla Freccero, eds., *Premodern Sexualities* (New York: Routledge, 1996), viii.

obvious, learn to decipher the proper missionary positions, go beneath the surface and you will find them, all worthy and playing both sides: Lancelot in love with his lieutenants, Rabelais more than equivocal with his ass-wipe, and—less than anecdotal—the great Flaubert himself, whose *gueuloir* in Normandy and book-about-nothing was positioned—or so we once thought—above all these little nuances. Discovering that in the Turkish baths in Egypt, it is considered good form to "run through one's boy in the chamber," he images, writing from Cairo to Louis Bouilhet at the beginning of 1850, "that it is one's duty to enjoy this type of ejaculation," which he ends up committing on the person "of a young fellow whose face was engraved with smallpox scars, and who wore an enormous white turban." He adds further on, as if to cheer up his old friend, that he "witnessed a week ago a street monkey leap upon a donkey and try to forcibly masturbate him." [2] These little indiscretions confirm that Gustave was one of our queer old uncles.

More generally, queer is the art of displacement, whether involving travel or animals, stylistics or bodies, the art of being where nothing awaits you. Besides the rich commentary they have provoked in the United States, the only point in common among the writers selected here is this traveling shot focused upon them that seeks out the elements that appear to be the most inoffensive, to the exclusion of the most suggestive ones. In other words, the approach does not aim to produce a homo corpus made of authors who would be "that way," nor an invert counter-corpus made of characters who, having denied it, can no longer escape the truth. We are looking for details that have been ignored, but then take on the sudden tumescent vigor of

---

2   Gustave Flaubert, *Correspondance* (Paris: Pléiade, 1972), vol. 1, 572-3 and 638.

that which passes through the glory hole.

For example, when it comes to medieval literature, we won't linger over the racy songs or the carnivalistic Saturnalias that have already been copiously studied. Instead, we will look into the virile friendships promoted by handsome Lancelot and the hermaphrodite echoes given them by queer critics. For the Renaissance and its dusty pens, we will pay less attention to the chaste link between Montaigne and La Boétie and more to the issues of their co-writing, less to Gargantua's dusky crack and more to the strange forms of Rabelais' monsters. In the case of Diderot's nun, less to the tender touches of the Mother Superior and more to the sexual ignorance that she fakes the entire time. As for the great libertines, enough has been said about Sade's sodomites and homo orgies; instead we'll look into the delays and small breakdowns featured in hetero coition. With Baudelaire and Théophile Gautier, less to their obsession with lesbians, well known enough, and more to the tactics they invent to slip from one sex to the other with the stroke of a pen. As for Balzac and company, less to the confirmed bachelors Vautrin and even Rubempré, and more to the shady playboys and gentleman cousins who never married. And finally, when it comes to Gide, Proust, and Genet—the official triad of homoeroticism—much less to Charlus, *Corydon* or the Montmartre fags, and more to the gestures that blur, all these peripheral oscillations that once and for all destroy the inept border between hetero and homo. A finger in your nose, as Roquentin could tell us, is sometimes richer in queer meaning than an entire session of fist fucking.

Everywhere, in a word, we will be looking into troubling separations rather than the less obscure pleasure of a clean intromission. Homosexuality, an overheated word if ever there was one, is not an object here, but rather a style, less a series of themes than the mobility that sets them in motion. Roland

Barthes, to whom queer critics have paid constant homage, suggested it many times over.[3] He believed that a text is not "homosexual" by its characters or its author, but only insofar as it presents itself as both object and subject of desire, the way it loves itself in the thrust of its deployment, "white" yet uncertain writing, the neuter that in *S/Z* goes beyond masculine and feminine, insofar as—in other words—it continually escapes, in its phrasings and plot, the sexual characterizations that psychoanalytic reading too often wishes to stifle into doctrine. To better understand this process of in(de)finite extension that queer critics call for, this lengthening of all lists not unlike the way the member pushes through the glory hole, we first need to comprehend what exactly is this American movement: what do we hear in queer?

---

3 Notably in his preface to *Tricks* by Renaud Camus (Paris: POL, 1988).

PERVERSE READINGS

> It granulates, grates, caresses,
> scrapes, cuts, and comes.
> —ROLAND BARTHES, *The Pleasure of the Text*

For every text, even secondary, its context. Before the homo-readings of literary texts could really take off on American campuses, a sociopolitical fight had to be won to effectively recognize a community, a struggle that we do not have to describe here, except to say that it has to be won each and every day. In 1969, the police attack on a gay bar in Sheridan Square set off the Stonewall Riot, and with it the political emergence of homosexuality on American soil, even before the American Psychiatric Association decided in 1973 to scratch homosexuality off its list of mental disorders, which gave it a more lasting legitimacy. But in 1982, the Bowers v. Hardwick affair once again set off political passions, in which a student (Hardwick) was caught performing sodomy in the pious state of Georgia, where the act can still cost you time in prison, nearly two centuries after the penalty was abolished in France. The Hardwick case—the Supreme Court made him a martyr in 1986 by upholding his conviction—was only one symptom among others, in the middle of a decade in which homo movements did battle with reactionary elites given comfort by the Reagan regime.

American universities owe the massive arrival of "minority studies"—gay studies, but also women's studies, various ethnic studies, and postcolonial studies—to this sad state of affairs. Little
by little, these areas of study were institutionalized as fields of
knowledge in their own right, creating research institutes and
accredited courses of study in the general curriculum. Around
the end of the 1980s, within the already wide field of homosexual
studies ("gay and lesbian studies"), we began to see an alternative development, quite dissident, that soon came together under
the banner of "queer theory," a name that feminist critic Teresa
de Lauretis was apparently the first to use in 1991. Dominated
by a handful of professors who soon became the divas of queer
fashion (most notably Eve Kosofsky Sedgwick, Michael Warner,
and Jonathan Goldberg), and inspired by the constant reference
to Foucault's *The History of Sexuality,* this new development denounced the dangers in the current approach's fervent quest for
identity which would ghettoize the very people it wanted to lib-
erate, and the residues of what it called "sexual essentialism," the
unspoken tendency to make homo and hetero, and also man and
woman, into natural classifications and eternal truths.

24

Disorienting the West
According to the nickname it picked up in America, a place where
lexical hybrids abound, "Queeory" had no small ambitions: nothing less than a Copernican revolution in sexual thought, another
way of thinking about sex. According to this theory, we needed
to oppose gay essentialism with the only "sexual constructivism"
according to which not only is the homo entirely the product of
other people's discourse (like the Jew, according to Sartre), but
heterosexuality itself, this "infamous obligation," is historically
only a consequence, a vague avatar of a more fundamental self-
eroticism that has always preceded the hetero/homo division.

Instead of homosexuality as a form, we need to substitute, with Foucault citations to back us up, homosexuality as a relationship, and as for homosexuality itself—much too conventional a thing with the psycho-medical discourse surrounding it from the previous century—we would much prefer the more exciting construct of a radical polysexuality. Like a seminal trace after the pleasure has gone, or the pleasure of the voyeur compared to those who are seen, queer is for its believers the name of a residue, what remains, both corporal and cognitive, surviving every attempt to pin it down, slipping between the cracks of dominant categories.

The queer approach, just as vague as the objects it unceasingly attempts to "dis-identify," loudly proclaims lack of definition as its major virtue. Its seduction is that of the veil; its magnetism, that of the ellipse. What the QCs share, according to William Turner, is this "tumultuous, boisterous, and unfocused adolescence" of knowledge, elusive and dispersed, its refusal to "settle into the adulthood of traditional disciplinarity."[4] The word "queer," that would be derived from the Indo-European *twerkw* (sideways), "connotes the crossing of borders," according to another of its experts, "but does not refer to anything in particular." It designates, says historian David Halperin, "*whatever* is at odds with the normal, the legitimate." In other words, in American homo-theoretical jargon, it demarcates "not a positivity but a positionality," open to anyone, gay or hetero, "who feels marginalized because of her or his sexual practices."[5] In order to be deliberately blurred, open to reaching heteros as well as the abstinent, swappers as well as fetishists, the queer *démarche* is not any less pugnacious, ready to reread the entire history of the West through the lens of this

4   William Turner, *A Genealogy of Queer Theory* (Philadelphia: Temple University Press, 2000), 9.

5   David Halperin, *Saint Foucault* (New York: Oxford University Press, 1995), 62.

all-important sense of suspicion. The entire Western episteme, in the Foucault-tinged terms of star commentator Eve Sedgwick, is "structured—indeed fractured—by a chronic, now endemic crisis of homo/heterosexual definition."[6]

Seen through this wide-angle lens, the very myth of the discovery of America, in the pioneer tradition, suddenly finds itself illuminated by a little known fact: the inaugural homophobic act by explorer Vasco Nuñez de Balboa who, upon landing in 1513, was to call down the dogs on dozens of Natives accused of sodomy and cross-dressing. Through sexual constraint, he colonized a continent that still needs to be liberated, and that for centuries to come will be defined by the primal confusion between front and back, that "preposterous" crime (the inversion, in this case, of procreation and anal pleasure) that, deeply offended, the aptly named British chronicler Peter Martyr described: "[Balboa] founde the house of this kynge infected with most abhominable and unnaturall lechery. For he founde the kynges brother and many other younge men in women's apparel, smoth & effeminately decked, which by the report of such as dwelte abowte hym, he abused with preposterous venus."[7] That's all it took for an incense bearer of the time to chronicle the great discoveries on the fingers of one hand and, later, for a queer historian to rewrite in his own way the tragic history of the Native peoples of America.

How to Take a Text

Much to the dismay of humanists and traditionally minded teach-

---

6   Eve Kosofsky Sedgwick, *Epistemology of the Closet* (Berkeley: University of California Press, 1990), 1. A change of tone in another opus where this time she queers education, offering several simple methods in "How to Bring your Kids up Gay," in Michael Warner, ed., *Fear of a Queer Planet* (Minneapolis: University of Minnesota Press, 1995), 69-81.

7   Quoted in Jonathan Goldberg, *Sodometries* (Stanford: Stanford University Press, 1996), 180.

ers, thanks to such efforts, the verb "to queer" has become transitive. In articles and presentations, people have started queering the history of the Union, lily-white advertising, TV sitcoms (Jerry Seinfeld being the very example of the "hetero-queer"), team sports, and the Bible itself. The classics of literature have been an obvious target, since in departments of the same name, this new fashion, like its predecessor, has conquered the greatest number of converts in the United States. Professors, always eager for new tags, started by pointing out the unexploited queer potential of peda-gogy, of textual anal-ysis, of works of f(r)iction, and the manipulation of short forms, Japanese, and Elizabethan texticules. On a more theoretical level, the first attempts at queer literary analysis set out a new concept of reading, a relation to the unestablished text, happily attacking the sad postulate of official critics, obsequious and heterocentric, according to which, as Lacan famously wrote of sexual relations, there are no textual relations. Instead, every text is ambiguous, hesitating over its sexual status, so say queer critics. We need to learn to *take* the text, *turn* it over, *penetrate* it, play with its sex, slip ours into it, follow it to the end of its fine ambivalence, and force it along the way to assume a position. There really is nothing new under the sun, or so it seems. In France, fifteen years before all this, wasn't Félix Guattari comparing our ways of "making love to Kafka" to our ways of "making love" to Joyce, Proust, and Henry James? Nothing new indeed, except for this complete sexualization of the act of reading, a detailed Kama Sutra of textual positions. The QCs assert that we first have to cruise the text to get to know it, then mingle our bodily fluids with those of the written work (our imagination with the semantic soft spots, our desire with the trembling of the sentences), read it head to tail to taste that textual sixty-nine; either that or turn a deaf ear to its song and engage in an ordinary session of reading masturbation. We need to experience the poem the way we would a quickie, a short story like a one-night stand, a novel like a serious affair, with its routines and its flaring up of passion.

In a word, let's forget about submitting to a text that would have a single meaning, the kind of thought we get from hetero critics with their dusty machismo, that kind of domination over a reader with feminine features by an aggressive, essentially masculine text.[8] According to that new kind of thinking, all reading is in itself sexual, but when compared to the power relations of ordinary reading—the dreary, obligatory missionary position—we prefer to substitute a more pliable and seductive approach that would "bring the text out of the closet to which the academy has long silenced it."[9] These metaphors of reading are sometimes at play in other fields than that of the sex act alone: geology is at work when a tectonic reading slowly breaks apart the text's underpinnings, producing earthquakes and lava flows;[10] and epidemiology: when it enters the fluid of a text's veins, better to instill a contagious infection in them,[11] or even torture in the words of critic James Creech, closer to the S/M sessions suggested earlier, if the reader is able to slice through the fibers of the text and commit violence upon its silky surface. In American university classrooms, these acts of daring have two consequences: one has to do with atmosphere, the other with vocabulary.

In the first case, try to imagine, in the long student-teacher tradition, the sexual tension that ran from the desks to the front of the room when the words "deep penetration of the text" were

---

8 For a more complete list of sexual metaphors of reading, see Mark Hawthorne, *Making It Ours: Queering the Canon* (New Orleans: University Press of the South, 1998), 23-26.

9 *Ibid.*, 97.

10 *Ibid.*, 114.

11 Jonathan Goldberg, *Sodometries, op cit.*, xvi.

pronounced. The tension was scholarly, yes, and could not be disassociated from the thousand pedagogical and literary references that helped it see the light of day, but that tension shook more than one professor (and both sexes were targets) who had the leisure to remark on it: "The reading aloud of a lesbo-erotic passage from Duras's *L'Amant* (evoking the sumptuous body of schoolfriend Hélène Lagonelle)," recalls professor Lucille Cairns, "ignited a mutual attraction between us which was to lie dormant until, as a fourth-year student, she did my Honour's option on French women's writing." [12] Unfortunately the story ends there, and we are left to use our imagination to picture their hot nights of reading.

Moving on, how to portray the relations between the masters with their rhetorical depravity and the timorous freshmen and freshly deflowered doctoral candidates who parade past, one after the other, under the complicit eye of their teacher, as they discourse about Marlowe's rectal grammar or the urinary allegory in Lamartine's work? The second consequence, as we have seen, is the rising up of a new lexicon, a code of affinities that would frighten our Sorbonne guardians. In that light, the aphoristic style becomes a "serial plenitude" (the repetition of thrusts); the end-of-century *flâneur*, a catamite on the prowl; the rhymed form, the flow of a homophonic hand upon the poetic member; the verb itself, a "copulative"; the sentence, a "paternal figure" to whom "the reader must show his backside"; and the preface and footnotes, "marginal spaces," of course. In a wider sense, the old division of stylistics courses ends up reformulated: denotation is a weapon of hetero monovalence, constraining, reproductive; and the connotative stands for the opening up of meanings and

---

12 See Lucille Cairns, "A Queer Romance: Me and French Studies," in *French Cultural Studies*, vol. 10, no. 3, 1999, 329.

senses, the loosening of the textual perineum, disquiet abandonment to its nameless delights, a very queer proposition in favor of
non-productive pleasure and sterile *jouissance*, or bliss. We can
see how queer critics, the children of Derrida as much as of Foucault—and they really have invented nothing new, but just intensified things—are less interested in the fullness of the text and
the objectivity of the context, and more in the contradictions and
lack of realism, silences, and analepses, all being discrete breach-
es in the hetero text, shatterings and anfractuosities, through
which the perverse reader and his homo polysemy might slip.

Inversion and Incompleteness

In the end, the queer relation to the literary text contains two
main ideas, both inseparable from a hypothesis about the primal
mobility of the sexes; two ideas that distinguish it from the traditional gay approach more clearly than those analytical word
games and the wider art of provocation. The first is involved with
a general reversibility of the sexes and positions, with inversion
understood as desubjectification; this is illustrated through all
queer literature by the obsessive fascination with the hermaphrodite—the androgyne, the hybrid, the cherub, the Nancy-boy,
the half-and-half, all figures of the double. Since "the function of
effeminacy, as a concept, is to police sexual categories, keeping
them pure,"[13] the queer critic wants to invert the tendency and return to the primordial sexual hesitation that precedes the impo-
sition of norms, which the relentless homophobic assault against
effeteness was trying to eradicate. The assault, so they would say,
that Aristotle himself launched in his *Nicomachean Ethics:* "For
effeminacy too is a kind of softness; such a man trails his cloak to
avoid the pain of lifting it." (Book VII, Section 7) Against Aristo-

---

13 Alan Sinfield, *The Wilde Century* (London: Cassell, 1994), 26.

tle's successors, the idea is to rehabilitate the long line of thinkers of the double body, tellers of androgynous tales, from Ovid's
Metamorphoses (wherein we are told of the burning and unpredictable relationship between Salmacis and Hermaphroditus),
up to Shakespeare's feminized Romeo, from Balzac's *Séraphita*
to George Sand's *Gabriel*, from Foucault evoking the "hermaph-
rodism of the soul" (an echo of the "spiritual fusion" from which
is born the androgyne of Antiquity) to the young Otto Weininger,   *31*
the Viennese psychiatrist and poet who committed suicide and
who, before Freud, gave credence to the idea of primal bisexuality,
and chose on that basis the only therapeutic nihilism.

The second level of queer reading, more political than this
cosmology of the hermaphrodite, refers to all the small modifica-
tions that the love of self introduces into the sex act: providential
onanism against the dogma of altruism and its obligation of mutual orgasm, the perversions of the unproductive against coitus
as a means to an end, the logic of the deferral and the unfinished,
those brief periods of waiting and frustrated caresses against
the simplistic teleology of insertion and withdrawal that results
from bodies that seem to consider pleasure as a kind of sneeze.
What fascinates the QCs are the great sexual failures in literature—shame-faced masturbators and deficient penises—and beyond that, everything that turns sex into a loss of self, against all
precepts of fashion and performance. And this to the point that
certain thinkers about homosexuality, such as Leo Bersani, accuse queer critics of being desexualized, unbodied, abstract, and
far too rhetorical, especially when it comes to the wholly organic
impulse hidden behind the fancy name of self-love.[14] If coming out
of the closet means only entering a space of language, a vague and
metaphorical space where bodies are less objects of desire than

---

14 Leo Bersani, *Homos* (Boston: Harvard University Press, 1996).

rhetorical figures, then the queer battle, certain homosexual critics maintain, will miss its target, having sidestepped, pen in hand and with a clean backside, that jouissance of which it is so proud.

The two transverse motifs of queer critics—the logic of deferral and the figure of the hermaphrodite—join hands within an esthetic that can be happily tracked throughout all literary works. This ostentatious, theatrical, and parodied esthetic of the wheezing old artifice and the over-the-top gesture, the flowery phrases, sophisticated till they squeal like the peals of laughter from drag queens, their fully self-accepting grotesquerie, their dripping makeup, their screechy voices—queer readers celebrate their hilarious bravery, the risk they take of ridiculing the body, the whole attitude famously summed up by the label "camp." [15] If everything can be "camp," from Proust's sentences to suburban garden decorations, if the label "queer" can swallow everything, beginning with that which resists it, we shouldn't be surprised if this new way of working has been applied over the last few years to the most varied cultural objects, and often the most unexpected. Robert Samuels wrote his jargon-filled *Hitchcock's Bi-Textuality*,[16] in which we journey through the wheelchair voyeurism of James Stewart and the secret of the man who knew too much, the salacious uses of the gag and rope and the wild ride of Eva Marie Saint and Cary Grant in *North by Northwest.* Less surprising are the queer exegeses of Josiane Balasko's film *French Twist,* with its vision of lesbianism seen through a heterosexual lens.

Meanwhile, colonialism has become a history of sexual slavery,

---

15 Susan Sontag wrote about this style long before queer fashion in her important collection *Against Interpretation and Other Essays* (New York: Farrar Straus & Giroux, 1966).

16 Robert Samuels, *Hitchcock's Bi-Textuality: Lacan, Feminism and Queer Theory* (Albany: State University of New York Press, 1998).

wherein indigenous feathers excite white desire, and the furs of the lieutenants' spouses do the same for the Native sorcerer. Not only has the French literary tradition been combed through, the Italian one has been as well, with its sodomite visions of hell taken from Dante's great frescos. And the Spanish version too, featuring the wanderings of Quixote and Sancho Panza, along with the German brand, for it seems that Werther's sufferings had a more specific cause than a vague ache in the soul.[17] These pleasure-bent readings add suppleness to German rectitude, discovering orgiastic echoes in the dialectic between master and slave, and even Gregor's metamorphosis in Kafka's short story features a monstrous coming out. The Romanian tradition isn't spared either, for it allowed the British Gothic writers, thanks to the myth of Dracula, that cape-wearing, solitary castle-dweller, to erect a statue to the greatest of all suckers. But before moving on to the homoerotic folds of the French corpus itself, to the storms brewing beneath the gentle countryside, let us quickly look at what queer critics have been able to unearth from the shelves of their own Anglo-American library.

33

17 In America lately, Goethe has been abundantly queered. See, among others, Alice Kuzniar, *Outing Goethe & His Age* (Stanford: Stanford University Press, 1996); and Robert Tobin, *Warm Brothers: Queer Theory and the Age of Goethe* (Philadelphia: University of Pennsylvania Press, 2000).

ANGLOFOLLIES

Then half Signor Benedick's tongue in Count John's mouth,
and half Count John's melancholy in Signor Benedick's face.
—WILLIAM SHAKESPEARE, *Much Ado about Nothing*

English or American? American literature not only constitutes
a less noble and narrower field of study on the campuses than
its British equivalent, it is less rarely the object of penetrating
readings that force apart the flesh of the text. Of course there are
traditional gay studies that celebrate a newly minted homosexual
corpus (from Edmund White to Allen Ginsberg, from Eileen Myles
to John Ashbery), but the major figures have yet to be queered:
Faulkner or Steinbeck, Pynchon or Dos Passos. It's true, F. Scott
Fitzgerald, when in his cups in Montparnasse, used to ask his
friend Hemingway to accompany him to the toilet to compare
the size of their manly organs, since Fitzgerald suspected his
was lacking. Beyond the simple anecdote, that story should have
awoken a glimmer in the eye of queer critics, who might have
considered how these great macho men of the pen played. Still,
Brit Lit represents a precious target for the QCs, more than their
various national literatures. The prestige of its history, the suspicious rectitude of its classics, the truculence of its shady characters but also the disturbances arising from the rituals it relates
(of workers or monarchists, men of the cloth or the colleges)—all

this turns the British corpus into a favorite playground for queer critics, who certainly wouldn't have seen the light of day without Shakespeare. This burning name, spelled by the essayist Richard Burt as "ShaXXXpeare," is the Open Sesame for all perverse readings, the rallying cry of all ambivalence—the uncontested jewel of the queer canon.

36 *ShaXXXpeare*

Be it comedy or tragedy, farce or classic drama, the permutations, hesitations, and sometimes the inversions of sex roles make the Shakespearian universe a veritable hothouse of queer figures which critics have been exploiting over the last twenty years. As we've seen, not only does Romeo rage against what he calls his femininity (that kept him, so he thinks, from saving his friend Mercutio), but Antony and Cleopatra, in the play of the same name, are depicted as two beings of the same sex, a double sex, a royal synthesis: the Emperor is not more masculine than the Queen of Egypt, nor is she more feminine than the powerful Caesar. The critic Simon Shepherd even tried to draw up a list, less than exhaustive, of instances of sexual indecision in Shakespeare's universe, a swarm of bisexuals, a garland of inverts, a cohort of nearly males: the court dandy, the king's favorite, the ticklish buffoon, the princesses' tailor, the submissive valet, the comrade-in-arms, the actor with his mumbo-jumbo, and even the poet, the subject of speech in whom the Sonnets show, for posterity, that this nascent subjectivity and scarcely latent homosexuality are inseparable. Yet, in Shakespeare's works, the availability of the secondary characters, a sort of sexual clay that can be molded into a shape that would please their masters, does not interest queer critics as much as the heroes' more troubling ambivalence, and that of heroism itself. If, in *Troilus and Cressida*, Patrocles becomes "Achilles' whore," his "male servant," in *Henry V,* the lords themselves, about to expire, embrace each other greed-ily, and not in search of a last breath of air. The critic Alan Sinfield beckons us to meditate on the "homo-necrophagic" story that the Duke of Exeter tells:

> Suffolk first died: and York, all haggled over, Comes to him,
> where he lay in gore ensteep'd, And takes him by the beard,
> and kisses the gashes. [...] So did he turn and over Suffolk's
> neck He threw his wounded arm and kiss'd his lips; And
> so espoused to death, with blood he seal'd A testament of
> noble-ending love. The pretty and sweet manner of it forced
> Those waters from me which I would have stopp'd.[18]

This portrayal of valiant warriors in bloody hand-to-hand battle here at Agincourt, thrown together in final embrace, seems to suggest, in the most facetious manner of comedies, a marriage scene. That's the situation of Lysander when he is trying, at the beginning of *A Midsummer Night's Dream,* to push aside his rival Demetrius who stands in the way en route to the beautiful Her-mia: "You have her father's love, Demetrius; Let me have Hermia's: do you marry him."[19] In order to get closer to power, the young barnyard rooster is forced to accept his virginal backside being assaulted by the virile thrusts of the all-powerful Egeus; the im-age of such a union—and here Lysander has it right—is as true as it is delightful. The recurrent model in Shakespeare's work of the tripartite love affair, a conflict among men for the honor (and body) of the same woman, is in other fields of queer criticism an example of the inversion of the poles of the triangle, a more dubious movement, when it's not a plain caricature. It's difficult,

---

18 William Shakespeare, *Henry V,* Act IV, Scene 6.

19 William Shakespeare, *A Midsummer's Night's Dream,* Act I, Scene 1.

in fact, even in one's wildest dreams, to imagine the irascible Othello less interested by the integrity of his spouse and the maintaining of the crown than by the rear end of the villainous Iago whom, according to some QCs, he'd like to run through with something other than his sword.

Then there's Hamlet's intriguing pallor, the same that Romeo displays when the woman in him appears, but that he replaces with the redness of rage. The pallor of a prince stretched between sexual poles; the pallor of the heir unable to assume his legacy; pallor, in any case, the queer exegetes tell us—and here they are unanimous—that can only be that of the onanist, in flight from the demands of History through self-satisfaction; pallor of the fine masturbator who would precede, in Shakespeare's work, a long line of compulsive heroes, aphasics, heroes of their own theater, each as pale as the sterile fluid they gush forth with, that solitary obsession to which British literature has given its stamp of nobility. Yet no polluter would go on to equal the ones of Shakespeare's plays: neither Marlowe's Tamburlaine who, several years later, suffers from moments of forgetfulness, nor in the next century Byron's demonic sufferers from melancholy like Manfred and Cain, whose unhealthy color seems to give credence to the doctors' theories and the censors of Onan. Nor those young lady mourners hotly tucked into their beds in Jane Austen's novels (to which the diva Eve Kosofsky Sedgwick dedicated her most famous article, "Jane Austen and the Masturbating Girl"), nor Dickens' "villains" who, like Uriah Heep in *David Copperfield,* display the "twisted dry hands" of those who use them a little too often. Nor, on the far side of the Atlantic (and the Hudson River), Philip Roth's fabulous Portnoy, who would break the record of twenty times a day, yet without ever reaching the tragic glory of the Danish onanist.

Besides the touching of oneself, the other queer series that

Shakespeare is supposed to have launched, and with it the entire British Renaissance, was nothing less than sodomy, "that confused category," as Foucault put it. But an enlightened sodomy, a knowledgeable ass-fuck that combined anus and knowledge in a kind of genuine rectalism, a little like the way Sade's "philosophers" brought together orgasm and rational discourse. Here, the queer term *par excellence* is "sodometry." In his essay of the same name, Jonathan Goldberg resuscitated this synonym of sodomy used in England in the sixteenth century, not only to turn it into an instrument to measure anal violence in several important English-language texts but, in a broader way, the very language of all British literature, of this corpus born from a land he mysteriously calls "Ailgna" (the warping of Anglia, perhaps?), this "always elsewhere, the home of sodomy."[20] The practice of sodomy, it must be pointed out, runs through both British history and literature like a true ritual and a foggy metaphor, two interchangeable registers for any self-respecting queer critic.

From Mollies to Dandies

After Shakespeare set it all in motion, according to the QCs, three centuries of queer culture followed, rich in caresses and cavils, disguises and disclosures—and not just brusque outbreaks of sodomy. First, Elizabethan theater features, at its end, a multiplicity of deviant figures: the cuckolded invert, the ambiguous "beau," the dandy with his furious gestures, a sexually polymorphous Knight Errant that Sir John Vanbrugh, in his play *The Relapse,* contrasts, as well he should, with real male heroes: "They are decent; he's a fop. They are sound; he's rotten. They are men, he's an ass."[21] Joining the old bisexual seducer of the British Renaissance comes,

---

20 *Sodometries, op. cit.,* xvi.

21 Quoted in Alan Sinfield, *The Wilde Century, op. cit.,* 35.

in the England of the early eighteenth century, the new figure of an exclusively homo sodomite, and a whole nascent culture of homoeroticism. The public attitudes of the "Mollies" attest to this; among their society, they imitate marriage and maternity with fake priests and rag dolls, but also, in a more repressive mode, the increasing denunciation of "gentlemen becoming girls," according to the enraged but soberly titled pamphlet published in 1749, *Several Simple Explanations for the Rise of Sodomy in England.* Wigs and makeup don't help things, since in London they became the indispensable signs of aristocracy and a feminine allure. Parody, itself the sign of a certain freedom, takes over as the queerest genre of the British Enlightenment. Even the great Shakespeare is not spared; his plays are transformed by, among others, Tobias Smolett, into drag queen cabaret shows before their time, where Anthony is wearing petticoats and Cleopatra armor. Meanwhile, far from the London of the Mollies, spinsters, poets, and solitary chroniclers, from the sixteenth to the eighteenth century, never stopped dreaming up worlds that erode normal borders. Thomas More's utopia, the paradise that Milton reinvented, and the island of Daniel Defoe's most recent Robinson: all were spaces of autonomy compared to regal England, places of extroversion in which "to satisfy his longing to be different" [22] (alone, or with Friday, or in a community...); enclaves that queer critics, two centuries on, would quickly associate with the homo closet—a cozy derogatory closet one does not wish to leave—or a sort of Rousseau-like Eden, queer style, as tenuous as the signs may be in these three canonic texts.

The British nineteenth century—industrial, colonial, and puritan—would perfect, in its margins, the confusion of genders, and constitute for queer critics the golden age of a certain

---

22 Mark Hawthorne, *op. cit.,* 58.

sexual indetermination. Yet that was the century when homophobia triumphed, launched in 1810 by the terrible repression of a
sodomite "coterie" on London's Vere Street, a group of "partners"
(among them, several tough guys, barge-drivers, and haulers of
coal, wearing classical whore's monikers) caught red-handed in
the midst of their pleasures and immediately expedited to the
pillory to be taunted by the good citizens of London. A society in
which a prole built like Hercules could go by the name of Fanny   *41*
Murray; a society on the threshold of which (in the elite Public
Schools) "Every boy of good looks had a female name, and was
recognized either as a public prostitute or as some bigger fellow's
'bitch'"[23]; a society that retained outside its proper commerce and
conjugal duty every possibility of mirrored pleasure. Such a society, queer critics insist, could only produce troubled literature,
shot through despite itself by the attraction of the same, all the
way to its least likely suspects, from Robert Louis Stevenson to
Rudyard Kipling (what do all those beasts in the jungle want from
that boy?), from Jane Austen to the Brontë sisters and, upstream
from a century of romanticism, from Jonathan Swift to the delicate Coleridge.

Beyond simple sexual preference, the figure of the dandy promoted by the salons of London, before Huysmans and Laforgue
refashioned the portrait—elegant, mannered, free-spirited but
asexual—brandishes the challenge of pleasure for its own sake,
of a mask soaked in indolence, against the spirit of virtue and
industry embodied by the Empire triumphant: vanity against
utility, art against commerce, role playing against role stasis and,
though menaced with the Victorian strap, the exploration of risk-
ier spots than the vagina with its promise of procreation—there

---

23 According to chronicler J. A. Symonds in 1850, quoted in Alan Sinfield, *op.
cit.*, 43.

we see, fully formed, the oppositions that will structure queer politics. By claiming a certain British affiliation, those politics will turn three scandalous authors from the beginning of the century, three avant-garde exiles who dared fence with the Crown, into three figureheads of the great homoerotic blur: Oscar Wilde, Virginia Woolf, and James Joyce.

Wilde, of course, for his dandyism, his esthetic of boredom, the courage of his tendencies, and his trial so richly commented upon, but also for the three queer archetypes offered up by *The Picture of Dorian Gray:* the artist of intensity (Basil Hallward), the dandy with the insouciant manners (Wotton) more feminine and decadent than the former, and their rare compromise (incarnated by Dorian), the alliance in a single individual—who is several beings, which is the point—of creativity and pure leisure, of the push for pleasure and the unfinished.[24] Then comes Virginia Woolf, whose enigmatic *Orlando* is still the most accomplished story about changing genders, a novel once celebrated by Félix Guattari as "the literary machine that produces changes of being," and today by the QCs because, by moving the character from "the masculine Augustan age to the Romantic Nineteenth-Century," the author shows better than any other "the art work's being hermaphroditic."[25] The preliminary sentence of the book can even pass for the transsexual gesture in itself, creating doubt by the very act of dissipating it (in a fictional parenthesis), and curiously linking androgyny to an act of decapitation: "He—for there could be no doubt of his sex, though the fashion of the time did something to disguise it—was in the act of slicing at the head of the Moor." A sentence like quicksand, which is to queer language what Boileau's counsel is to French: matrix, refrain, proverbial reference.

---

24 See Alan Sinfield, *op. cit.,* 98-100.

25 Mark Hawthorne, *op. cit.,* 100-101.

And finally we get to James Joyce. His queer streak is both more generous and less specific; throughout his work, the wandering body abandons itself, whether it's Bloom's scatophilic wanderings or Stephen's zoophagic brand. Both open onto a universe of generalized confusion between animal and phallic tails, between seed and excrement, creation and prostitution, for these are just several elements in Stephen's dark dream in *Portrait of the Artist,* with its masturbatory orgies and the swing of filthy phalluses. Though not enough of a classic narrative to lend itself to perverse reading (yet too risqué to be sullied further), Joyce is less useful on American college campuses than Virginia Woolf, and Woolf herself is the exclusive property (a bit paradoxically) of lesbian theoreticians, less studied in her queer version than undeniable Oscar, the veritable measuring stick of all that is queer in literature since homo-reading appeared.

On the other side of the Channel, in the French corpus, the same attention is paid to Montaigne, Diderot, Balzac, Baudelaire, Gide, and Proust. Around them, like a queer serpent coiling around the Edenic trunk of some hetero tree, the unanswered Wildean question of sexual oscillation turns, the ironic interrogation that the writer offers, still moist with embrace, about gender inversion. Faced with its silence, we'll put this question to the French corpus, unrolling it chronologically as we said we would, to watch it slowly swell into a crisis of certainty—sexual and textual. For the blasé naturalism of our most recent contemporaries is only a late-coming avatar of that crisis, and here I'm thinking, to name three French authors of today, of Michel Houellebecq's quadriplegic swappers, Guillaume Dustan's showy displays of dildos and poppers, and the refined swooning in the parking lot as told by Virginie Despentes.

DRAG QUEENS AT BOUVINES

> Toward him he turns when called
> And with such virtue do they come together
> They kiss so strongly and clasp each other so sweetly [...]
> That their stirrups break, and both fall in the meadow.
> —ANONYMOUS, *Ami et Amile*

Poor Middle Ages: unjustly decried, its poetry reduced to the ballads of troubadours, its vision to monkish scholasticism, the sensations of its population to the rough hair shirt against the skin and the squirt of boiling oil on a helmet. There again, American critics have done salutary work, rehabilitating corpuses that grim humanism had strapped into submission, unearthing pearls of postures hidden in epics too quickly skimmed, and meeting each year in a town in Michigan to celebrate, with wine-tastings and processions of dwarves (be they fantasy or not), the brilliance of "medieval studies." From colloquium to round table, the queer axis of a new version of the Middle Ages more daring than what our masters were willing to admit is developed from semester to semester. The *Fabliaux* take on an air of gay pride; Guillaume de Machaut's voice begins sounding like that of a castrato, and his "fountain of love" more like a golden shower. Illuminated manuscripts suddenly begin teaching us about the art of representing the genitals, Christine de Pisan's Ganymede becomes a "guardian of the closet," the *Évangile des Quenouilles* and certain of Marie de France's Lais morph into lesbian odes, and the Spanish Inquisition itself, with all due respect for its victims, turns into the murderous transference of the desire for sodomy.[26] Homosexuality such as we conceive of it now had no meaning back then (nor right to exist), for sodomy among men led straight to the stake. The hero of *Du sot chevalier* isn't queer enough to risk being taken by *le cort batre* (assaulted through the short hole—the anus), and Guillaume de Loris in his *Roman de la rose* warns of the dangers that threaten the rear guard, and even has one of his characters proclaim that he would prefer to be "hung on a cross" than fall victim to so cowardly an assault.

But as Foucault so clearly demonstrated, the flowering of discourses about sex, if only to regiment its practice, made it a radically omnipresent object through direct desire and literary imagination. The medical discourse of the high Middle Ages, queer critics remind us, is not the least explicit. It attributes the pleasure some males experience through sodomy to a twisted urethra (carrying the seed to the anus instead of expelling it), and it scientifically sets down the method of healthy coitus, as did the thirteenth-century *Régime du corps* authored by Aldobrandino of Siena, the ancestor of our Masters & Johnson. Religious traditions are no less erogenous, whether they be the inaugural *possesso* of the new Pope, during which God's representative on earth would sit on a throne with a hole in it so his genitals could be ceremoniously examined, thereby avoiding a repetition of Pope Joan's dishonorable deceit (according to historian Richard Ingersoll), or even the polymorphous imagery of Christ on the

---

26 To cite only a few examples from the colloquium entitled "Queer Middle Ages," held in November 1998 at the City University of New York.

Cross, of which the medievalist Karma Lochrie wrote—seriously, we imagine—that "the wound of Christ is one aspect of the feminization of Christ's body, and it exists in a representational nexus of a woman's vulva and vagina." [27]

What's more, military ritual adds an additional disturbing queer layer: the rites of knighting reproduced on lordly shields wherein a robed character to whom homage is rendered occupies the lady's place in a courtly scene, armor over the crotch which swells the genitals, or with the layer protecting the torso clinging to the pectorals. But according to the same logic of cross-dressing, it also seems to be hiding a feminine breast. Then there are the accoutrements of knights at repose (delicate tunics, unlaced sandals, flowing hair, manicured nails); as far back as 1130, Saint Bernard feared that such things were less "a warrior's protection than the trinkets of a lascivious woman," [28] a complete ambiguous panoply overseen, as it turns out, by their ladies-in-waiting. These different examples, especially those that suggest the paradox of the coquettish knight, are brandished by queer critics. In varying ways, these examples confirm such critics' central hypothesis concerning medieval culture and its French refinements: the hypothesis of a constant inversion of sex roles, an ostentatious mobility between feminine and masculine that would constitute the major motif of medieval literature, where it is not rare to see knights swearing eternal love to each other with greater fidelity than to their ladies, and not without caresses. Meanwhile, the ladies are decking themselves out in warriors' outfits, like that warlike Parisian woman who attracted the ire of Gilles d'Orléans in 1273, who declared in an ardent sermon that she "is so well equipped,

47

---

27 See Karma Lochrie, "Mystical Acts, Queer Tendencies," in Karma Lochrie, *et al.*, eds., *Constructing Medieval Sexuality* (Minneapolis: University of Minnesota Press, 1997), 194.

28 Quoted in *ibid.*, 116.

from head to toe, that she breathes the fire of the devil [...] [wrapping] her middle with a silken belt," better to hide her feminine curves.[29] This inversion of roles explains to some degree the success of the different versions of *Lancelot* among queer medievalists, and the profusion of perfidious details that they discover to back up their assertions.

Lancelot Uncovered

Rather than examine one of the sources often cited—*The Knight of the Cart*, attributed to Chrétien de Troyes—we have thought it better to look at the most complete version of the anonymous prose work *Lancelot du lac* from circa 1225. The opening descriptions of the "poor unknown knight" create ripples of emotion among the QCs. Before even unholstering their interpretive arsenal, they dreamily savor the image of Lancelot at age eighteen, "completely armed, with helmet laced, shield hanging from his neck, and with his sword girt on." When he is presented to the court, his portrait, no less tasty, includes a certain number of feminine touches: the small mouth and silky neck that, had he been a beautiful damsel, would not have been out of place. Then comes the knighting of Lancelot by Queen Guinevere, with Lancelot entirely covered in shining armor except for his hands and head, a phallic knight freshly uncovered at the feet of his benefactress. But the homo-reading of Lancelot focuses on his relation with the knight Gawain who is not simply the go-between, even if he does make the bridge between Guinevere and the mysterious knight, though not without telling the Queen, "I give you this knight for all time, though he was mine first."

The American critics are not the only ones to have explored the homoerotic content of this exclusive camaraderie in arms,

---

29 Quoted in *ibid.*, 128.

beginning first with a violent joust between the two men, which they quickly put to a stop in order to embrace one another and swear fealty. The historian Jean Markale and the medievalist Christiane Marchello-Nizia have questioned this "virile love," though Jacques Roubaud preferred to see in it the more platonic avatars of a "melancholy Eros." But queer readers and their plethora of commentaries add to it the beauty of hermeneutic drifting, trapping slowly but surely in their nets everything that is not clearly explained. Language, here, risks leading them into errors, since the French "Galehout" becomes "Galehot" in English, creating a link between the two companions via the sounds of their names, the mirroring and rhyming of them, two identical endings, spherical and erectile, short and piercing.

49

More seriously, there are abundant signs throughout the story—if signs can be said to be credible—pointing to a relationship between Lancelot and Galehot that is closer to courtly love than simple comradeship, more like the spoken desire for promiscuity than a banal oath of chivalry, though the ardent adventure remains chaste, for medieval appearances demanded it. In love at first sight, Galehot totally falls for Lancelot, gives up his world and freedom for him in the tradition of *fine amor,* and even swears to give him everything if he agrees to share his tent, to shelter him a night, risking his refusal and discreetly joining him, after he has fallen asleep, for the sole pleasure of listening to him breathe. King Arthur is not wrong when he believes that, when it comes to Lancelot, Galehot is more jealous than a knight with his damsel. Nothing surprising, then, that he dies of sadness three days after the announcement—erroneous, alas—of his friend's death on the field of battle. Add on a little mimesis according to the well-oiled model of "the desire for desire," and our first great story in the vernacular all but turns into an orgy for three.

Not only does the knight Gawain declare in public that he is ready to become his "devoted virgin" to win the enviable companionship of Lancelot the way Galehot did, but the latter agrees to be betrothed to the Lady of Malohaut in order to imitate Lancelot's love for Queen Guinevere, without the subtext revealing anything of a foursome. In the United States, the debate is on over whether, between the two knights, there exists an anachronistic "homosexuality," or a more chaste "homosociality"—unless Galehot's feelings arise from the former and Lancelot's from the latter. Supporting the first hypothesis are those who cite Galehot's recurring attacks, spasms, and weeping in the presence of such a delicate partner. Supporting the second is the negative role, in the final analysis, that their liaison plays into the economy of the story, since it keeps Lancelot from conquering the Holy Grail. The critic Gretchen Mieszkowski defends the first thesis,[30] whereas the medievalist Reginald Hyatte answers with the second.[31] Hesitating between the two, Jane Burns leaves the question open as to whether Lancelot is more a "ladies' man" or a "lady/man."[32] Whatever the case may be, the bond between the two men runs through women: as they lie side by side of a warm summer's night, they speak softly of their respective affairs. This is a decent pretext for intimacy between men according to hard-core thinking, or simply intimacy in general (and not specifically homosexual) in the softer version.

Textual or sexual, rhetoric or erotic, the *masculine amicitia perfecta* is no less a classic part of stories of chivalry. This be-

30 Gretchen Mieszkowski, "The Prose *Lancelot*'s Galehot, Malohaut, Gauvain, and the Queering of Late Medieval Literature," in *Arthuriana*, vol. 5, no. 1, 1995, 21-51.

31 Reginald Hyatte, "Reading Affective Companionship in the Prose *Lancelot*," in *Neophilologus*, vol. 83, no. 1, 1999, 19-32.

32 Jane Burns, "Refashioning Courtly Love: Lancelot as Ladies' Man or Lady/Man?" in Karma Lochrie *et al.*, eds., *Constructing Medieval Sexuality, op. cit.*

gan in the twelfth century with the *Roman de Thèbes* in which the two heroes, Tydée and Polynice, declare their love for each other through verse after verse, until the latter attempts out of spited love, on the former's tomb, to run himself through with his own sword. That's also the case around 1200 with the anonymous *Ami et Amile* that describes to a T the furious embraces, whether standing in their stirrups or lying in a meadow, of the two valiant knights of the title. For the Middle Ages, the ardor of companions-in-arms is but one of the possible forms of a more general blurring of sexual identities. According to queer critics, three other commonly discussed figures enter into play here: the lady-man, the transvestite saint, and the mythical hermaphrodite.

51

Heiress, Saint, Hermaphrodite

The thirteenth-century *Roman de Silence,* attributed to a certain Heldris de Cornuälle, invented a human creation that fascinates queer theorists: the male without a phallus. Since the law forbids women to inherit property, Eufémie and Cador decide to disguise their daughter Silence, from the beginning of her young life, as a boy, hoping she will actually become one. Silence will play her role zealously, winning every tournament, juggling like an expert, charming the damsels, and even receiving a title from the King of France, to whom the inevitable Merlin will finally reveal the hoax.[33] More charmed than deceived, the monarch will leave his queen in the final scene to ask for Silence's hand. Working with motifs of shame and dissimulation, the *Roman de Silence* illustrates the central thesis of the philosopher Judith Butler, destroyer of sexual categories, and another indispensable queer reference, according to whom sexual gender is not an essence but a theater of expression.

---

33 See Elizabeth Waters, "The Third Path: Alternative Sex, Alternative Gender in *Le Roman de Silence*," in *Arthuriana*, vol. 7, no. 2, 1997, 35-46, from which the quotations are taken.

For her, sexual identity is constituted only by the performance of certain forms of expression that are then presented as the result.[34] If other heroines of the time, most notably Blanchandine in *Tristan de Nanteuil* and Yde in *Yde et Olive,* support Butler's thesis long before it was set down by "becoming" the men they imitate, more than any other heroine, Silence troubles queer readers because of her talent for inventing a sex for herself.

Gay deception is at work here on every level. The text points out that Silence "still has only flour in her pants": a bit of flour applied to the bottom of her pudendum and molded into her linen underthings will perfectly simulate the genital swell of the medieval macho. Silence is so well cut and buffed, thanks to her long work-outs, that she uses her physique to repel the advances of various princesses: "I have a mouth too hard for kissing, and arms too rough for embracing." In a very rare occurrence for the Middle Ages, Queen Eufême, irritated at being rejected by Silence, accuses her of being a man's man: "He is a homosexual, I know it for certain." Her husband the King, more inventive, uses gender-neutral forms to speak of her: "creature," "being," "person." Still, "the boy-maiden" (a phrase often cited on American college campuses) divides American critics. Instead of the transgressive power of a complete change of gender, others see the stock denouement that in the end reinforces hegemonic norms.[35] Still others conjure up the delights of a third sex, the substitution of a "neither/nor" instead of a simple "this/that." In any case, the story's ending represents the victory of queer confusionism: "Here we have a romance in which the king ends up marrying his favorite knight and where the good woman (Silence) is preferred to the

---

34 Judith Butler, *Gender Trouble: Feminism and the Subversion of Identity* (New York, Routledge, 1994).

35 *Ibid.*, 135.

bad woman (a queen) because she was a good man!"[36]

Another queer figure of the high Middle Ages is the "sacred virgin," the canonized nun. Here again, from Sade's monasteries to Roland Barthes' commentary on Loyola, the beastly odor of isolated convents has been celebrated in French before. But the QCs drive the nail home: the diffuse sexuality that hovers around the forbidden, the bodily violence implied by asceticism, the trance brought on by constant communion with one's Savior—all these factors heated up the cool corridors of the cloisters. Under the pretext of a more complete outlawing of those unspeakable twin globes, more than one monkish treatise offers mouth-watering descriptions of women's breasts. Certain nuns did in fact illegally change sex in order to escape masculine desire and the libidinal clamoring of the pagans beyond the gates, not to mention the lascivious gazes of friars at their forbidden objects. In other words, to remain virgins, the faithful brides of Christ at times put on men's clothing, the only guarantee of their sexual integrity.

The hagiographies of several saintly women who cross-dressed out of love for the Lord have since become choice pieces for the queer corpus. They start with Saint Euphrosine, a sister who became a monk and in the convent took on the male name Esmérade. To protect herself against the priapic assault of her fiancé who wished to hurry into marriage, so moved was he by "her gracious small breasts," Euphrosine asked her father permission to take holy vows. He agreed. But she had not anticipated the libido of those churchmen, just as excited by the seductive nun who made herself up as a man and began frequenting the monastery as they were by the "nubile eunuch" who prayed along with them. Luckily there were more conventional priests, but they preferred

---

36 Simon Gaunt, "Straight Minds/'Queer' Wishes in Old French Hagiography," in Louise Fradenburg and Cara Freccero, eds., *Premodern Sexualities, op. cit.*, 166.

to damn that "Satanic castrato" rather than their brothers of the cloth. For a "man" with such feminine airs to so titillate the monks is of greater interest to the queer critics, of course, than the more banal friction of co-ed convents. These critics triumphantly produce the conclusion that these cases of cross-dressed saints "show the extent to which all gender roles are performative, imitations of an absent model."[37]

In the end, from Galehot courting Lancelot to saintly ladies disguised as saintly men to banish their breasts, not to mention the edifying example of Joan of Arc, whose cross-dressing and not her war-making led her to be burned at the stake, medieval literature provides queer critics with less of a repertory of catalogued caresses, and more a rich combination of sexual roles, a whirlpool of permutations—more chaste but also more playful than the more recent corpus; and more suggestive because it is more indirect, like a giant game of blind man's bluff wherein the contestants would not even have the right to touch. That's why the queer figure par excellence of the French Middle Ages is not the lesbian princess or the generously endowed knight, but the hermaphrodite—the major enigma that these centuries of magic would hand down to the more rational eras that followed. At the end of the Middle Ages, this monster of origins, an obsessive hybrid myth, would give free reign to the anatomical drift that the more courageous QCs would work to discover in the epic novels. They found it more gratifying, instead of rereading pastorals and other trifles (and who can blame them), to concern themselves with the treatise of Ambroise Paré, *Des monstres et des prodiges* (1573), or to leaf through *Discours sur les hermaphrodites* (1614) by Dr. Jean Riolan, or the treatise by the same name penned by a certain Jacques Duval (1612).

---

37 *Ibid.*, 165.

The critics love those minute descriptions, with anatomical cross-sections on full display, of sodomites disqualified from the manly role by the memory of the vagina they owned at birth, or female androgynes whose genital appendage is in fact a giant clitoris, swollen enough to be a penis, or those frightful interregnum creatures with both sexes, a stifled scrotum hanging down over the beginnings of a uterine opening. In the pages of serious academic journals, queer analysis licks its chops over the celebrated cases of sexual duplicity in France at the time. There was the case of Marie le Marcis (1601), accused under the name of Marin of repeatedly sodomizing the maidservant Jeanne Le Febvre, and saved from the stake by the expert witness Dr. Duval, who demonstrated that his/her member emerged from the vagina—she had one of those too—only if he was "duly stimulated" (it must have functioned perfectly well, since he apparently made the maidservant come "four or five times in the night"). Then there was the case of Marguerite Malaure (1686), a pretty lady from Toulouse whom the magistrates of the city declared a hermaphrodite and forced to wear the clothes and bear the name of Arnaud Malaure. In the end she pleaded her case before the king himself who, aided by his doctors' expertise in anatomy, granted the gentleman a woman's identity.[38]

Since the erotic jumps quickly to the theoretical, queer critics have updated the issues in the discussions of the times about hermaphrodites as the very debate in which they are most involved. The question is whether sexual identity refers to a binary model of origins, or whether, on the contrary, it is distributed in a more random manner, and less naturally determined, according to the innumerable degrees along a polysexual axis. The latter

38 According to Lorraine Daston and Katharine Park, "The Hermaphrodite and the Orders of Nature," in Louise Fradenburg and Carla Freccero, eds., *Premodern Sexualities, op. cit.,* 124-127.

option, of course, enjoys all their favors. These are two incompatible hypotheses that will battle it out during the French Middle Ages. The first, derived from Aristotle's *The History of Animals,* attributes the existence of hermaphrodites to a supplement of intra-uterine "maternal matter" that, insufficient to produce a twin, adds an extra member (either external or internal) to the first fetus, without denying the idea of an original separation of the two sexes. The second, more ancient, issues from the writings of Hippocrates. Through a certain number of chance factors (the quality of the seed, the position of the egg in the uterus, etc.), it explains the possibility that between man and woman—and against the postulation of their dichotomy—a series of intermediaries are born, and it is up to medieval exegetes to determine whether they are children of God or monsters to cast out. This veritable Hippocratic cameo of sexual identities represents, for queer logic, the promise of a multiplication of pleasures and erogenous zones, as well as the opportunity to rehabilitate the somber Middle Ages into something like a period of relative freedom that has since been lost as sexual identities have been more clearly assigned. As for that freedom, the following period—the French Renaissance—did not abandon it, and even added, much to the pleasure of queer readers, some most unusual stylistic leaps into a *writing of disturbance.*

RENAISSANCE AND (DE)TUMESCENCE

> His codpiece [...] hath an erective virtue and comfortative of
> the natural member.
>
> —RABELAIS, *Gargantua*

It is tempting to credit queer critics with a counter-history of
French literature, a term-by-term inversion of the chronological
standards we all learned in college. The Middle Ages appear
richer in deviances than the boring humanist century (and richer
still than the *Grand Siècle* with its police), were we to judge by
the attraction that Pascal and Boileau, or Montaigne and Rabelais, exercise on the QCs. Given the small number of queer articles
that it has inspired in the New World, the eighteenth century, so
pleasantly liberated, seems less rich in ambivalence than the century that followed. There is indeed an imbalance, from the point
of view of the queer critic, between these roughly cut slabs of literary history, but to conclude that there is an objective inequal-
ity between texts from different periods (more tendentious, or
polysemic, in certain centuries than in others) would be to mis-
understand the characteristic lack of definition that queer ways
of reading use. The energy of reading counts more than its result, and the unexpected enriches it with surprising pathways;

sometimes, works less adjusted to its way of seeing don't always lead to the best discoveries.

The sixteenth century offers the most appropriate illustration. The flowering of new genres, the emergence of reflection about the self, the increase in feminine writing, and the creative homage to the Greek masters created a space of literary renewal, a renewal of themes and styles, licenses and concepts, within which, at first glance, queer reading seems ill at ease, as if its ambiguities had become redundant, its textual assaults unnecessary to the revelation of a disturbance quite well described by the humanists in page after page. On the other hand, these critics are fully interested in Villon's hanged man, Ronsard's roses, De Bellay's wanderings, and the veritable manifesto of sexual resistance—according to some of these readers—known as Marguerite de Navarre's *Heptaméron* (1558), whose author apparently invented a sense of sisterhood and feminine mockery of the court seducer. But like the Devil in Scripture, Old Scratch is always hiding where we least expect him. We just need to explore the classics of this new era a little more deeply to find, according to the QCs, motifs that are less queer *per se* but more obscurely ambiguous than the passion of "friendship" in Montaigne, Pantagruel's suspicious bachelorhood, and Madame de La Fayette's criss-crossing desires—while staying within these three canonical authors' works.

Montaigne Entwined

Don't worry: Montaigne the intimate, the free-thinking author, the suave being whom so many readers cherished like a brother, can never be transformed into a furious sodomite or even an apostle of sexual ambivalence. Distrustful of the pleasures of the flesh, content that the celebrated "Greek license [was] justly abhorred by our manners," declaring that women (whose "soul does not seem firm enough" to him) are incapable of "responding to the call and communication" of true friendship, Montaigne doesn't offer much purchase to perverse reading. Though he does declare that "many men, especially in Turkey, go naked out of devotion," this is not the call of his heart; he is more like an ethnographer who wants to clothe the natives. If the world is but an "endless cesspit," the upright man may have nothing to do with it. Though he did praise to the skies the "tight and durable knot" that bound him for four years to Étienne de la Boétie (until the latter's early death), Montaigne's *Essays* (1580) display no sign of sexualizing his tender and lyrical concept of friendship. The rare bodily metaphors in the chapter "On Friendship" refer at best to a vague sort of telepathy, or at worst to a "spiritual pleasure" that he says he reached with the young author of *Discourse on Voluntary Servitude.* "At our first meeting, we found ourselves so captivated, so familiar, so bound to one another, that from that time nothing was closer to either than each was to the other." Their souls alone "seemed to blend one into the other, doing away forever with the seam that had joined them together." Is this the fault of the Hellenic embrace? To be "simply founded on external beauty," far from this "loving recommendation" that lifts their entente to reach "this constant and complete warmth, all smoothness and gentleness, with nothing bitter or that would cause friction," quite the contrary of married passion or rectal intrusion. Étienne's body is completely absent from the text, since it is the body of "the one who is not the other," of he who offers him "the miracle of becoming two," the joy of being "the second in all things," than the inconsolable sadness of "being only half a being"—a factorial friendship, an algebra of affect that the queer critics attempt to transform into a union of bodies.

If we are going to queer Montaigne, we'll have to look elsewhere, a degree above the banal turpitudes that the man himself resists. For critic Jeff Marsten, the homoerotic relation is not directly what binds Montaigne to La Boétie—no matter what indiscreet biographers think—but is instead what binds the text between friendship and the writing of the self. From this second relation, textual in nature, emerges the "collaboration" of the two writers such as Montaigne's homage describes it. From his pen flow the twisted, crafty criss-crossing of texts, embracing, interpenetrating, a common winding together and reciprocal insertion, a subtle assembling of their prose; Montaigne's autobiographical notes enveloping La Boétie's political ideas, a story of friendship suddenly mixed in with the author's remarks about the public reaction to his friend's treatise. We can never clearly separate the two spaces within the text; so closely associated are they that they form the image of a paper hybrid, a double work or at least "more than individual," against the authorial authority invented by this first century of the individual. Above all facile metaphors, two texts melt into one another, exchange their fluids in the way that other, more simple-minded critics imagine the two men doing; the way that Montaigne himself did all through his work with the bodies of texts of Raymond Sebon or Lucretius, Seneca or Cicero. There, in that interlacing—in that acquaintanceship of texts, a wandering sentence, indolent or more chiseled—is where queer critics like to reread the *Essays*.

This mania for digression, so dear to our first great wanderer of the pen (who begins one chapter by comparing the three sorts of wind expelled by the human body), becomes in itself a major queer motif, "the trope of dilation," according to Patricia Parker, a way for critic Robert Martin "to defer, to distend, to prolong, like foreplay repeated until it becomes the act itself." The relation to the self launched by the *Essays* is in itself a solipsism of pleasure and an autarky of generation, as much a titillation of the self that might be compared to masturbation whose completion is always put off—a solitary caress illustrated by Montaigne's many formulations, beginning with the famous "I bask in myself"—as the suggestion "that his body is pregnant with its own text" that "must in a sense give birth to itself," from delay to digression, as Julia Watson has put it.[39] The queer content of the *Essays*, more abstract than Rabelais' craftiness or the future orgies of the libertines, consists, in a word, in the author's refusal—a refusal as stoic as it is homoerotic—to come out of himself, to penetrate the world, to reduce its mystery through the efficiency of a single meaning. A mere brush brings it into being: "I must lightly caress the world," said Montaigne four centuries before the QCs, "and not break upon it."

61

The Temptations of Dr. Rabelais

Rabelais' work doesn't seem to lend itself to the indiscretions of queer reading, but for the exact opposite reasons of those we saw in Montaigne. Instead of knowing winks, the title characters of *The Life of Gargantua and of Pantagruel* (c. 1532) exhibit hearty truculence, a straight-ahead lustiness that deactivates the old "repressive hypothesis" (to use Foucault's term) that queer criticism postulates as the source of every great text. Here again, the ambivalent zones appear where we least expect them, in a shadowy area away from the most explicit shenanigans, turning the latter on their head to discover a more disturbing face. Next to Pantagruel's outbursts and Panurge's tricks, "the great love" they declare for one another (Chapter 9) and the jealous, exclusive "friendship pair" they come to form is closer to medieval companionship or even Greek liaisons—since they compare themselves to Aeneas and Achates—than the spiritual bond between

---

39 In Patrick Henry, ed., *Approaches to Teaching Montaigne's Essays* (New York: The Modern Language Association of America, 1994), 128.

Montaigne and La Boétie. More troubling than Gargantua's size is the metonymical slippage that takes place in Chapter 8, the subject being apparel: slippage from his "codpiece" presented as sparkling with emeralds and rubies to what it covers, since it cannot be just a piece of cloth when it is described in an endless sentence as "that horn of abundance, it was still gallant, succulent, droppy, sappy, flowering, pithy, lively, always flourishing, always fructifying, full of juice, full of flower, full of fruit, and all manner of delight," nor a simple detail of his accoutrements in regards to the pleasure he takes by exhibiting it: "I avow God, it would have done one good to have seen him."

Then a second slippage follows, from the gargantuesque organ to a mythical member with its own autonomous life, free of the subject that would own it, a queerer penis in its independence than the banal attribute of the eponymous giant. Whether codpiece or what lurks behind it, the governesses embellish it each day "with fine ribbons and beautiful flowers," allowing it "to return to their hands," naming it "with a thousand names" (rod, or vermillion sausage). The outlandishly graphic quality of Rabelais' text is not really at issue here. What strikes the queer ear here is the confusion between the container (the codpiece) and the contents (the member), and later between the latter and young Gargantua himself—granted the status of a mythically endowed child—against the mercantilist hierarchies characteristic of clothing (this border between the body that must be hidden and a prosperous industry) and even of the "natural member." Whereas the latter is supposed to be the property of the subject, his jealous capital, the private domain of a human person, here it tends to replace the person, becoming itself the supreme being under the cover of several amusing jokes.

The celebrated "Picrochol Wars," the carnage of separated shoulder blades and "unhanded hamstrings," become themselves

the objects of a second-level reading. The heroes' murderous pleasure and the author's more verbal variety interest the queer critic
less than the shared pleasure that Gargantua and Friar John experience while disemboweling their enemies, the pleasure of bring-
ing their bodies together to the rhythm of massacre, in the end using tender nicknames to encourage one another: "my sweet," my
"little monarchette," or even "my little ball-sac." The same verbal
riot is perfectly observable in the famous "torcheculative" chapter
(Chapter 12). The explosion of energy that Gargantua expends in
order to find the ideal way of wiping himself, moving from a hood
to a lady's neckerchief, from a cat to his mother's gloves, from
gourd-leaves to the living room carpet, reveals less the quest for
an irreproachably clean hind end and more the sudden discovery, with violent abandon, of the unequaled sensitivity of the anal
area. The "gentle-woman's velvet mask" has neither hygienic nor
transgressive virtues, but, as he says, the divine "softness of the
silk was very voluptuous and pleasant to my fundament." Finally
he reaches for "the neck of a goose, that is well downed," whose
warmth and softness fulfills his rectum with "the felicity of the
heroes and demigods in the Elysian fields." Focusing in on these
small displacements of Rabelais' text, these slight slippages of
the hero's desires (from a clean ass, here, to an ass of pleasure),
American critics have credited Rabelais with a true revolution of
the body, the *ontological* project, to use a mighty word, of a total
body, a fusion of both sexes and all functions, much more than
the sweet-tempered transgressions that humanist reading finds.
Scatology, confirms Jerome Schwartz, becomes eschatology here,
and excess the radical erosion of all our borders.[40]

---

40 See Jerome Schwartz, "Scatology and Eschatology in Gargantua's
   Androgyne Device" (quoted in Margaret Ferguson, *et al.*, eds., *Rewriting
   the Renaissance: The Discourse of Sexual Difference in Early Modern Europe*
   (Chicago: University of Chicago Press, 1986), 147.

The QCs' meticulous efforts to excavate the hermaphrodite motif in a work that very rarely mentions it (except for the recurring joke of "the beast with two backs") turn Rabelais into the typical object of queer micro-reading, and the example of an interpretation as picky in its analysis as it is delirious in its conclusions. In that same Chapter 8 about Gargantua's accoutrements, Rabelais briefly describes a golden badge his hero wears on the lapels of his tunic:

64

> A fair piece enamelled, wherein was portrayed a man's body
> with two heads, looking towards one another, four arms,
> four feet, two arses, such as Plato, in Symposio, says was
> the mystical beginning of man's nature ...

Critic Carla Freccero dedicates a prolific article to this passage.[41] Her goal is not to show that Rabelais has indirectly but incontestably assimilated his most famous character to the hermaphrodite of ancient myths—quite the accomplishment for an author whom feminists accuse of being misogynous and gays of latent homophobia. The middle scale of a closed text doesn't interest the critic here (the fair mid-point formed by every individual work according to our humanist masters), but rather the infinitely large and infinitely small, drawn from just a few words. Talking about the infinitely vast, the meaning Freccero gives this passage goes much further than the mere study of the work. With the same logic we saw among queer medievalists, Freccero has Rabelais rehabilitating, against all Platonic idealism, the more materialist thesis of Hippocrates and Aristophanes according to which human beings' sexual origins would have a "self-sufficient third

---

41 Carla Freccero, "The Other and the Same: The Image of the Hermaphrodite in Rabelais," in Margaret Ferguson *et al., op. cit.*, 145-158.

term"—a creature that has disappeared, Aristophanes believed, leaving us only the name: the hermaphrodite—a being half-male, half-female, "formed like a globe," with a "cylindrical neck" and equipped with four arms, four legs, two backs, and two sexual organs. A being, Freccero insists, who, by its ability to give itself pleasure, would incarnate the love of self, the great alternative to the earlier myth of Adam and Eve.

So much for the queer politicization of pre-Socratic myths. As for the infinitely small, it is to be found in one of the most re- markable bits of bravado in all queer criticism: Freccero's bold analysis of two little words in French, *virée vers* (for the hybrid being's two heads) translated in English as "looking towards." According to this critic, Rabelais could just as well have written *tournée vers* ("turned towards"), so it's no accident that he opted for the alliteration of *vir/ver,* the phonetic echo of *vit,* the French word for "penis." The alliterative sound effect of the virile mem- ber would be a way, according to Freccero, of rereading the myth of Aristophanes in the sense of *masculine* love of self, of excluding the vulva from the hybrid of origins. Not to mention that, accord- ing to certain medieval lexicon specialists, the French verb *virer* referred to, in the fifteenth century, the pelvic rotation that pre- cedes sodomy between men and that, etymologically, the suffix "-ire" designated at the time an arrow or a stick, a clearly phallic protuberance. What's more, says Freccero victoriously, the lit- eral meaning of *virer* signified at the time the action of turning around what is presented to us face first. In other words, four lines from Gargantua, or more to the point, three syllables within those lines, support the queer hypothesis of a male homosexual reinterpretation of the myth of the hermaphrodite by the here- tofore unsuspected Rabelais, and the idea that his hero would wear on his lapel, hidden by the icon reproduced therein and with the codes of the times, the slogan of the sodomite origins of humanity. Since we come from it, why not return there?

Trouble in the Clèves Family

After the writing of the self and the Gulliverian epic (re)inventions of the Renaissance, the classical period ushers in another major genre with the psychological novel. *La Princesse de Clèves* by Madame de La Fayette (1678) is a masterpiece of the genre.

In the absence of clear bodily clues, with the princess seeking shelter in a convent rather than offering herself to the duke, the queer reading of Nemours's amours is more indirect, more an allusion, a soft brushing, more superficial at times than the reading of Rabelais or even old Montaigne. But enough vigilance—let's follow the meanings uncovered. Certain critics see the beautiful demoiselle de Chartres, who has become Madame de Clèves, as a "protofeminist heroine" who manages to dodge the constraints of marriage, this marriage of respect (more than of reason) that binds her to the boring Clèves, and outwit the patriarchal codes of the court of Henri II. Other analysts have turned her into the victim of the "traffic in women" that is part of aristocratic society, and the source of her "emotional anguish and physical solitude" [42] in the novel. Her situation is fragile and her lucidity strong, a typical alloy of queer uncertainty. Her sexual abstinence, and the liaison with Nemours that is all the more platonic insofar as they see each other only three times during the story, takes on a value of resistance. This is the silent denunciation of a fools' market, a macho court where women pay while lying on their backs.

Homo-readers are quicker to direct their attention to the masculine characters. Insofar as the rules of the aristocratic game put men in competition with each other to win the favors of the

---

42 Lewis Seifert, "Masculinity in *La Princesse de Clèves*," in *Approaches to Teaching Madame de La Fayette's La Princesse de Clèves* (New York: Modern Language Association of America, 1998), 60.

ladies of the moment, a familiar triangle is sketched out by the QCs: the triangle of competing desire, a reciprocal irritation of two men in a mirror, a male itch of two strike forces. A triangle, in other words, that according to queer rereading, uses the female object as a pretext for the friction between two virilities.[43] That's the case, rather more athletically, when it comes to Nemours and the Chevalier de Guise, and rather more flaccidly between Nemours and Monsieur de Clèves: the loser's fatal melancholy for the latter and physical distance from his belle for the former, who is reduced to secretly obtaining, then admiring in solitude, a portrait of the princess. Both men are portrayed as a pair of impotent heteros who, if only they came out of the closet, might gain some ardor—except that, to the great displeasure of the QCs, the Alcibiades-style suite to *La Princesse de Clèves* has yet to be written.

Here again, two versions face off with each other. A softer one, wherein the critic is happy concluding that a homosocial relation exists; and a harder one, wherein the mediation of the female body—her image in the stolen portrait, or her furtive appearance in the palace corridors—serves only as a sexual stimulus, a fetishistic switch, a more fundamental homoerotic bond, though it cannot come out through Madame de La Fayette's pen. Besides, and more credibly, Nemours and Clèves, because they are the first two masculine heroes to lose control of themselves because of heartbreak, are in the avant-garde of a future cohort of trembling heroes, the pioneers in a long line of weepy phalluses, men split asunder. Their torments strip them of their virility, their tears make them effeminate, the preciousness the author displays when speaking of their affliction wraps their muscled bodies in a new form of weakness. The way emotion and uncertainty rule their lives, excluding of virile reason, transforms them (though

---

43 *Ibid.*, 63-65.

they don't realize it, of course) into the first critics of the sexual Manichaeism that was in full flight then, as if they were invalidating ahead of time the coarse picture of a world divided between strong men and weak women.

Setting out to mock this very French melancholy, the British writer Nathaniel Lee—and here let us pay homage to Anglia's nancy-boys—surpassed, three centuries previous, the queer readings of the novel, taking full measure of these diminished males, these hard-hearted court-warriors softened by their femininity. Under the title *The Princess of Cleves,* in 1683 he offered the London public a parody stage version of the French intrigue. His play opened with a tender exchange of words between the Duke of Nemours and his servant Bellamore: "My cherished heart, my sweet well of love, my spouse, my Ganymede." It then went on to praise masculine grace, the virtue of men of emotions, as well as the youth of these strapping fellows. This of course constitutes a reduction of Madame de La Fayette's masterpiece, and of the boldness of certain queer readings, by seizing upon the motif of the foppish male, as well as the old-fashioned British buffoonery whose only merit was to uncover a second identity of the court seducer—that of the secret invert. A laudable merit since, at the threshold of a new century, this mocking Lee and his uproarious farce cast sudden doubt over those wigged ladies' men, and in so doing, a bit of shadow over the imminent Age of Enlightenment a few years before its arrival.

THE LIBERTINES OF FUCK-ALL

> When, instead of helping the male member to engage with
> its vaginal refuge, the palm constrains it to circumscribe
> and to stroke an armpit, a buttock, an ear—blasphemy.
> —JEAN-FRANÇOIS LYOTARD, *Libidinal Economy*

The ascetic Grand Siècle was followed by the sexual license of the
Enlightenment, at least as far as the elites were concerned. Like
a child let loose in a toy store, the first reaction of queer critics
when faced with the libertine profusion of the eighteenth century,
with its masters and scoundrels, its orgies and "philosophers,"
was to not know where to start—and to want ever more as they
unearthed homoeroticism in texts that were the least explicit.
Rather than interest themselves in the aristocratic chapels, historically admitted, that the century consecrated to the love of
self—from the Order of the Sodomites to the Society of Friends
of Crièce, not to mention the more Sapphic Vestals of Venus—they
preferred to exhibit much less direct and more furtive embraces.
For starters, there was the rumor according to which Voltaire had
a homosexual experience during his stay at the Court of Frederick
II, or the brief passage in *Candide* that evokes the habits of the Bul-
gars (or "buggers," an old synonym for sodomy, bearing out the
prejudice that the vice came from elsewhere), or even the cult of

admission and "difference" under whose sign Rousseau opened his *Confessions*—before admitting in Book II that he'd unwittingly caused an orgasm in a Moor who was very attracted by him.[44] The bisexual rites of the masters in Sade or those who inhabit the more scalding novels of forbidden literature—*Le Portier des Chartreux* or *La Tourière des Carmélites,* for example—have been the object of an overly general brand of study, having been dissected for years now by conventional criticism and classical exegetes. As a result, queer critics have looked elsewhere.

Once again, queer critics, protecting their love of detours, have preferred to throw up a smokescreen and direct our gaze toward the lower edges, the shadowy passages of that great orgy that was the Enlightenment, a little too overexposed for these critics' liking. They are less prolific when it comes to the eighteenth century, too showily indecent, than the nineteenth century or even the Middle Ages. Still in all, from article to essay, they are quick to point out the "failings" that make the great prerevolutionary orgy suspect in their eyes, the courtiers' embrace as much as the literary sporting. The double aspect of the great figures of the century who, when faced with masculine sodomy, boast of their own tolerance but still label it an "incident" (Voltaire), a "crime against nature" (Montesquieu), or a "bodily vice" (Rousseau). Then comes the denunciation through satire and medical injunction of this shameful accident known as impotence, "the first sign of some great malady" (Voltaire in his *Encyclopédie*), proof if we needed it that at the dawn of bourgeois trade, all that counted was coital performance and penetrating efficiency, ruling out all

---

44 See Jacob Stockinger, "Homosexuality and the French Enlightenment," in George Stambolian and Elaine Marks, eds., *Homosexualities and French Literature: Cultural Contexts/Critical Texts* (Ithaca, NY: Cornell University Press, 1990), 162-169.

unproductive caresses and laughable failures.[45] Then, following the same logic, we reach the apology of sexual performance and heterocentric coital productivity, a virile doctrine that helped create our contemporary mechanisms of "control of the body" (Foucault) through sexual health—a doctrine that fills queer thinkers of all stripes with horror.

The QCs choose to reread our eighteenth century outside this rather theatrical sexual competition. They do so by suggesting, in accordance with their favorite triangle such as the one found in *Les Liaisons dangereuses,* on one hand Valmont's desire for the firm buttocks of his competitor Danceny, and on the other Merteuil's longing for the roseate intimacy of her little protégée Volanges. Along similar lines, in *Manon Lescaut,* the parallel "friendships" of the Chevalier des Grieux seem suspect to these critics. They deviate our own reading of Sade toward the queerer motif of *ennui,* or boredom, that springs from the terrible monotony illustrated by the endless lists contained in Duclos' daily relations in *The 120 Days of Sodom.* And again, the abandonment of all will is a much queerer theme in Boyer d'Argens' *Thérèse philosophe* than the appearance of lurid turgescence. Hence, in that story we have the erect *Pater* ordering the fervent Éradice, as he labors her flesh out of the love of God: "Forget yourself and let it happen." Sticking with the examples that we ourselves will explore in writers such as Rétif de La Bretonne and Crébillon, these critics restore nobility to the themes of the detumescent male and deferred pleasure, and by examining those light-handed nuns they will discover the

---

45 The demonizing of the failing penis along with the frigid woman is a religious heritage of the sixteenth century that considered that those who "tie off their matchstick" were bad Christians [Yves Citton, *Impuissances: défaillances masculines et pouvoir politique de Montaigne à Stendhal* (Paris: Aubier, 1994), 156-158]. We were freely inspired by his remarks for the queer analysis of Crébillon that follows.

major theme—largely misunderstood—of sexual ignorance.

The Feints of Crébillon

More frivolous than Rousseau, less systematic than Sade, Claude-Prosper Jolyot de Crébillon, in dialogues and novels, constantly featured small ambiguities, like a constellation of queer falling stars, gaily fleeting, in the brilliant firmament of a century of sexual affirmation. He whom Diderot named, barely disguised in his book *The Indiscreet Jewels*, "Girgito the twisted," did in fact practice an indirect, wandering style, enjoying periphrases to the point of chatter, quite the opposite of the Ciceronian phrasings of Rousseau, or the more graphic descriptions of the divine Marquis. Rather then celebrating instances of happy coition, Crébillon's *Sylphe* (1730) lingered over the ethereal autoeroticism of solitary noblewomen, exploring their bodies amid the dreamlike flight of little winged phalluses. *La nuit et le moment* from 1755 presents the dialogue between two characters, Clitandre and Cidalise, who are psychologically blurry and just as vague as their words. Their talky obsession with setbacks and the opportune moment does not exactly make them furious indulgers in the present tense of pleasure. Texts as diverse as *Ah, quel conte!*, *Atalzaïde*, and especially *Le Sopha*—which we will look into here—feature, just at the moment when carefully prepared desire should triumph, scenes of impotency which Crébillon—though he doesn't own the monopoly on them—will refine to a greater degree than his contemporaries (as his antecedents, we could point to Bussy-Rabutin and Fougeret de Montbron). Even as he introduces us into the heart of accomplished libertinage, with overheated bodies and minds in vagabondage, Crébillon includes what many of his fellows refused to look into: the detour, the verbal feint, the delay, the caress without penetration, and, of course, the dramatic fiasco.

Published in 1742, *Le Sopha* takes its inspiration from Middle Eastern-style erotic tales that appeared by the dozens ever since the arrival of the *Thousand and One Nights*. Bougeon made fun of the fashion as early as 1733, imagining a country that had succumbed to the charm of a single book, where a thousand and one bookstores were taken over by stories of harems with extravagant titles, the *Thousand and One Quarter Hours,* the *Thousand and One Furors,* or even the *Five Hundred Mornings and a Half.* Crébillon's tale picks up the theme, that already has queer accents, from the anonymous *Canapé couleur de feu* (1714), in which Chevalier Commode becomes this particular piece of furniture after having drawn a blank with the repulsive fairy Crapaudine, the deformed and wrinkled inverted image of the gallant ladies of the Régence. In *Le Sopha*, set in the mythical city of Agra, the hero Amanzéi is punished by being tuned into a sofa. His soul will forever inhabit this comfortable place of reclining, doomed to observe from very close range the sporting of successive couples, tales he will immediately tell the Sultan. Here is a flimsily disguised portrait of the French court well known for its swapping, in which the onanist Louis XV had the scandals of the previous day read to him every evening from the police blotter. *Le Sopha* displays a criss-cross of a number of queer themes: at the origin of the fable, a double switch (that of Persian tales and that of the licentious scurrilous satire mocking court life); at the level of plot, a double voyeurism (the one Amanzéi engages in and the one he provides the reader).

Thanks to a parade of feverish lovers who are no less loquacious, we receive a direct account of the hypocrisy and gallant masks that lead to the satisfaction of personal desire. In the personage of Amanzéi, there is a disturbing metamorphosis that blurs the borders of the sexual individual. Besides becoming a sofa, he was a woman in a past life, which makes for a tasty triptych enjoyed by Crébillon. Along with more conventional lovers like Almaïde and Moclès, or even more sincere ones like the tender Phénime and the timid Zulma, the few failures who spend time on the sofa provide the most disturbing scenes in the queer meaning of the term. At the top of the list is the foppish Mazulhim, a repeat wet noodle. Though he enjoys the reputation of an irresistible seducer and indefatigable cocksman, when it comes time to perform, he has to slip his sword back in its sheath, despite the ardor of the sensual Zéphis and the graceful Zulica. "The most sought-after man in Agra," cackles Crébillon, "[...] is plagued by a weak heart." Yet from the queer perspective, the great mastery of foreplay and the burning descriptions brought on by the frustrations of his beautiful would-be partners suggest, against a negative concept of masculine failure, the alternative of substitute pleasures, the multitude of sophisticated caresses not involving penetration, not to mention the ecstatic pain of unfulfillment—whether Crébillon (or less so Mazulhim) is aware of it or not. Impotency is no longer just the loss of control, but the opening onto a field of perversions. The libertine lexicon backs up this idea by offering a failed double image to every term designed to designate the plenitude of desire: *overwhelm, languish, trouble, weakness,* and *excess* voluptuousness—in other words, exceeding the coital imperative, and not just good manners.

The infinite extension of delay, characteristic of so much of Crébillon's sporting, can be interpreted in the same way. Following what Yves Citton calls the "logic of the generalized missed opportunity," lovers in Crébillon's work, as well as in many scenes of the libertine corpus, seem to be constantly out of synch, one chatting away while the other is dying to do it, and vice versa. It's a little like that cartoon by the French satirist Reiser (at the risk of darkening the Enlightenment with such a frivolous reference) in which a jovial mayor tries to marry off Mr. Come-Too-Quick with Madame Can't-Come. Here, the principle of complementar-

74

ity that makes for efficient heterosexual relations is ridiculed. "To be perfectly happy in love," says Atalzaïde in another Crébillon novel, "our sex would always know pleasure, and yours, never." This admission of incompatibility is music to queer critics' ears. "Do everything to me," the object of desire seems to beg with increasing intensity, as the initial harmony gives way to the less sharable anxiety of a demand doomed to remain unsatisfied. "Do everything to me," repeats the object of desire to he or she who is but a weak subject, a limited fop, poorly rigged out, duped by the fashionable doctrine of an alliance of impulses: the weakness of the organs that "embarrass" a soul (or a libido) with its ambitions, the sexual thirst of the libertine (of either sex) proportionate only to the dissatisfaction that is his or her destiny, objectless desire that "dies only when it is fulfilled," as the Mole puts it in Crébillon's *L'écumoire.* This recurring formulation checks in whenever Crébillon's erotic display begins upping the ante. Like many licentious authors, he clamors for "always more," a constant postponing that, from level to level, slowly loses sight of its goal and its means to reach it. This formulation leads to queer suspicion, to a corrosive homo-reading within seemingly triumphant libertinage. Not at all a negative reading—perfidious satisfaction faced with such dissatisfaction—but an equally positive reading that sees unfinishing and unaccomplishment as something other than their sad prefixes. Here enters the opportunity to explore unknown zones, to try out a desire that will not simply fall away, to eroticize the entirety of the social body. Crébillon and, before him, the Taoist erotic treatises saw therein a motif of health and, when you think about it, why not?

To keep inside oneself, at the tip of the penis or the base of the perineum, that primal itch without trying to scratch it (or destroy it) with a harmony of bodies, with the illusion of another: that is the program of queer erotics, perisexual or even masturbatory;

a painful caress, if ever queer exegetes could produce an effective erotics. The literary rehabilitation of sexual failure includes an issue more directly queer insofar as it destroys several main axioms of hetero love—or at least its Christian altruism. From the *Fabliaux* to Rousseau, from badinage to sweet talk, from Crébillon to Stendhal's famous *Armance*, impotency travels through our literary history. Its queer readers, taking on the mantle of therapists, beckon us not only to remove the drama from it, against the romanticism of a *fatum* of breakdown, but, in a deeper sense, to be proud of it. Instead of the official fresco of a turgescent military marching off to simultaneous orgasms, we can read in pages once too quickly skimmed less pompous canvases, and more pleasurable in their own way, of indifferent openings, half-erections, softened tools, and happy digressions. The true turn of the screw is elsewhere, the writer would have said.

The Nun Who Knew Too Much

Crébillon and other libertine polygraphs were busy building an altar to pleasure with divine caresses, bodies possessed, immaterial voyeurs, even confessions of impotence elegantly dramatized wherein, deprived of his sword, the penitent seemed to echo Jesus's doubt on the Cross: "My Lord, why have you forsaken me?" Meanwhile, Diderot was sexualizing the sacred, or at least illustrating by the slightest wanderings of the body the metaphysical questioning of his time: knowledge, faith, freedom. With *The Nun* (published posthumously in 1796)—logically enough the work of reference for queer critics—Diderot, the most consistent materialist of his generation, instead of turning to the theater of swooning—after all, we're in a convent here, not in one of Sade's cults—prefers the details of glimpsed emotion, set in an austere cell, but described with more precision than the strenuous bouncing on the sofa. The scene is stripped bare; forget about the heavy draperies and Persian palaces. Few bodies cross paths here, far from the multitudes found in this sort of novel. The intimate focus bears on a few simple issues, frightening in their range, and on a discussion among a small committee. At a crossroads in a corridor in the convent of Sainte-Eutrope, there is only *you* (meaning each reader, the only one of his kind), the new recruit named Suzanne Simonin, the troubling mother superior, and, in the distant mists—between two monstrous mammaries sculpted into the cloister columns—the author in his observation post, standing less for God, because of his position outside, and more for his tempting Absence.

What occurs is but yesterday's memory, narrated in a low voice like a confession given the morning after, but with the nervous slowness of the most crucial scenes, the most debated of the queer corpus—hundreds of pages have been devoted to scrutinizing and analyzing one scene that is no more than a brushing past, including those penned by the high priestess of queer, Eve Kosovsky Sedgwick.[46] What is going on here? Interrupting their conversation, the mother superior lifts her skirts, places Suzanne's hand between her legs, demands that she kiss her forehead, her eyes, her lips, and moves her fingers as she feverishly runs her own hands over every part of the younger woman's body, sobbing now as she begs her in a strange voice to give her greater caresses. Then, pale as death, her eyes closed, her lips tightly sealed, though a curious pearl of foam has blossomed there, a violent spasm suddenly overcomes her, and her lifeless body drops to the ground. That's it. That is Suzanne's story, and it is far from the banal embrace of a tribe of coifs. There will certainly be other suspect moments, such as when the mother superior accords Su-

---

46 See the first chapter, "Privilege of Unknowing: Diderot's *The Nun*," in her book *Tendencies* (Durham: Duke University Press, 1993), 23-51.

zanne the "favor" of taking her into her bed, but everything is already present in that first scene.

Here, "queer" refers to a displacement, not that of furtive caresses, not even that of homosexual pleasure. It is a displacement of the conscience, visibly outdone, toward an excess of the body; displacement of the act that Suzanne literally does not *comprehend*, toward the incongruity of its effects—unknown sensations she cannot decipher, those frightening "convulsions" of her superior, the sleepy lethargy that overtakes them both after the spasm, a fatigue that Suzanne had "never felt in the middle of the day." But, just as Rousseau is suspect with his silly claims that he understood nothing of his Moor's trembling, what does Suzanne's *incomprehension* really mean? Are we meant to believe her, since her ignorance doesn't prevent her from being devilishly efficient, and her burning body cannot help but remind her from time to time in the solitude of her cell? Diderot's allusions to onanist practices and the sensual touches of his most proper nuns are not there to mock the religion of the defrocked, as Sade does throughout his tales; they are there to ask a more troubling question that would obsess Foucault and, after him, every queer theoretician: what does *knowing*, or not knowing, mean in sexual matters? The duplicity of words, Sedgwick answers, blows apart our little theater of signs. That famous "innocence" designates both a purity before desire and an appetite for pleasure not yet formulated. It points to that sacrosanct "ignorance," a virginity of the soul before representation (how to desire something if we don't have its image?) and a docile quality that increases pleasure.

As for "naïveté" itself, it stands for primary irresponsibility and, why not, a diabolical trick. The queer project is to give these terms a sexual positivity against the moralism of a lost paradise that sees them only in a negative light (ignorance before knowledge, naïveté before its corruption, innocence before it's too late).

It doesn't matter whether Suzanne is duplicitous; her body knows what's up when her skin begins to tingle and her nipples spring erect, and those low cries that come from somewhere inside her, the sudden moisture of her netherlips no matter how prudish she is, and the lips her mother superior usually uses to speak to her. The homonymy of *lips*—those for coming and those for speaking—destroys the humanist barrier between conscience and libido, so say the QCs. To the devil the negative: to not know means excluding oneself from the domain of guilt, reaffirming pleasure, making oneself irresistible to the other's body (even more so with a body of the same sex), and being able to play on all the meanings of the verb "manipulate," passive when her superior corrupts her, active when she herself is ready to put her hands to the task. Suzanne is not a "victim," say the QCs, moved by her sweet virginal body. She stands at the crossroads of knowledge and ignorance, their singular combination makes her an unequaled apostle of pleasure.

To queer the libertine century means setting aside the more athletic texts, since they're too showy to tease anything new out of them. Instead, let us slide a curious hand between the lines of the more hesitant stories, more sober, wherein tiny details or a seemingly innocuous gesture send our sexual certitudes into greater confusion than the exotic positions of Thérèse or Juliette's burning embers. Crébillon's impotent lovers and Diderot's innocents represent a happy detour on the road to pleasure which is often too crowded in the Age of the Enlightenment: the detour of a certain desexualization, drooping dicks and purity of soul, built upon the ruins of the official pleasure dome, the dwelling of hetero athletes and wigged marquis, another less "natural" sexuality, more uncertain and less binary, more extensive. Of course there's always Sade, but strangely enough the QCs have avoided him so far, and besides, he's hardly a vibrant apostle of sexual health. Some of the questions he asks—about the destruction of the other as a rule of pleasure, and the mathematics of bodies more subtle than the hetero axiom of $1 + 1 = 1$; or about prostitution as the only response to sentimentality—these issues are formulated in other ways, in other contexts, by several of the great authors of the century that followed, a century more bourgeois than aristocratic, more inverted than amiably open.

THE BOURGEOISIE OF THE INVERTED

> To fuck is to aspire to enter another,
> whereas the artist never leaves himself.
> —BAUDELAIRE, *My Heart Laid Bare*

What would our geniuses from 150 years ago look like were they to be lasciviously sent through the glory hole of our reading? Be it a metaphor for a pleasurable reading or a true opening in a stained partition, the celebrated orifice suddenly appears too narrow for Maupassant's legendary member, Balzac's meaty philosopher's hands, Rimbaud's rotting leg, and Baudelaire's refusal to copulate. With all respect for physiognomists, this century of great protuberances lends itself best of all to the game of queer mirroring; that is, as long as we forget their self-satisfied posturing and concentrate instead on their more insidious missteps or, rather, measure the former with the yardstick of the latter. In literature as elsewhere, modernity—a simplistic label that emerged around the middle of the nineteenth century between romantics and naturalists—has a taste for the impossible that absolutely delights queer critics. Modernity in itself tends toward those places of obscurity where such critics love to immerse themselves, that inner tension of an Ideal that has tragically fallen into the abyss of subjectivity, like an overly ambitious cocksman who, by the end of the night, has been reduced to a pitiful carcass, polluting the sheets in order to fall into a serene sleep. Modernity sketches out a road that never arrives, a constellation of crevasses, disappearing into detours, an obsessive road all the same, far from our postmodern mode of being blasé and athletically inert. The false steps that, all along the way, line after line, propel our great pen-pushers with their wild manes away from their Absolute goal so noble in its intent (the total novel, poetic communion, objective history: all hetero illusions of a century so tragically queer); those steps have made the nineteenth-century Republic of Letters the preferred playground of queer exegetes, who have found endless arguments against hetero dogma in that period.

In the tormented landscape of that century, they encounter an embarrassment of riches: there is Balzac celebrating castrati (*Sarrasine*), George Sand androgynes (*Gabriel*), Théodore de Banville hermaphrodites (with his 1867 collection of the same name), and even Mallarmé with the obscure embrace of two nymphs in "The Afternoon of a Faun." A number of male writers turn to lesbian fantasies that are anything but ethereal. Think of Baudelaire's lascivious soul mates and Flaubert's joyful assertion: *"Madame Bovary, c'est moi."* Meanwhile, Verlaine was aiming his weapon at Rimbaud. From the salon to the cenacle, dandies and followers of Jeune-France, dilettantes and the damned make both woman and sterility flower within them, as later in the century the unpredictable Des Esseintes of Huysmans' creation and the directionless *flâneurs* of Jules Laforgue will do. And even if Zola, above all suspicion, appears to escape the wave of uncertain sex despite the Sapphic dyads that dot his trajectory (Nana and Satin in *Nana*, Suzanne Haffner and the Marquise d'Espanet in *La curée*), the QCs seize upon this opportunity to tarnish his coat-of-arms: did not the honorable novelist stubbornly refuse that Italian invert who contacted him and suggested he turn his double life into a story of sexual vertigo? Zola's biographers have forgotten all about that refusal, but when jumped on by new American readers, it takes on the status of a major revelation about naturalist ambivalence, much more than the emblematic value of a biographical anecdote.[47] Still, it would be difficult to spot a latent inversion of the sexes in the story of the Rougon-Macquart clan, or dream of the innocent caresses of the miners' children sitting on slag-heaps, or the sly siestas of department store salesgirls; *Germinal* and *Au bonheur des dames* have resisted queer assault till this very day.

This is the great century of cross-dressing. Like in the nightmare of some virile charmer, drag queens are everywhere, from History to sonnets, from the penny dreadfuls to shadowy sidewalks. Their limp gesticulations and parody squeals alter this fine era—the dawn of bourgeois marriage, sexuated and hetero—and threaten to put in its stead, lugubrious and laughable, the twilight of masculinity. Queer readers even see drag queens in the proper works of Alexandre Dumas *père*, for did he not choose, at the end of the 1820s, to dedicate his first two historical dramas, *Henri III et sa cour* and the troubled *Christine*, to two monarchs reputed for their homosexual attractions? First up was the rather floppy *Henri III* draped in the toga of the times, in the back of which certain readers imagine a discreet opening for furtive sodomy. Then came the irascible Christina of Sweden got up in warrior's gear. In the middle of the Restoration, with its impotent kinglets and plush aristocrats, Dumas grants the royal figure a new languor: "The validating symbol of traditional patriarchal authority," concludes Adrian Kiemander, "is occupied by the figure of

---

47 See Vernon Rosario, "*Histoires d'inversion*: Novelizing Homosexuality at the Fin-de-Siècle," in Dominique Fisher and Lawrence Schehr, eds., *Articulations of Difference: Gender Studies and Writing in French* (Stanford, CA: Stanford University Press, 1997), 100-118.

a capricious woman or a sodomitical drag queen."[48] At the first performance of *Henri III* at the Théâtre français, a year before Hernani hit the stage, there were stories about young theater-goers who, emboldened by these inverted monarchs, staged an improvised dance around the busts of Racine and Voltaire, shouting, "Racine *enfoncé*! Voltaire *enfoncé*!" Enfoncé, here, means "impaled," making it clear, according to the QCs, that everyone understood the anal implications of the two plays. But unlike England, wherein illegal sodomy was the rule, the French nineteenth century belonged to tribades rather than mustaches; the caress of the hands rather than the rectum. This was the century of the troubled woman (she who desires to become the male author but also, as in books, she who disguises herself as a man) more than the virile homosexual.

In this perspective, the crucial novel is none other, for many critics, than *Mademoiselle de Maupin* by Théophile Gautier (1835). Even its famous preface has become a reference in the queer corpus, less for its call to scandalize the bourgeoisie and more for its delicate esthetic of "art for art's sake." In the same family as young Silence from the Middle Ages or a Joan of Arc revisited, Madeleine de Maupin changes herself into Théodore de Sérannes, motivated by a very queer curiosity for masculine life, as well as the desire to enjoy its privileges. The sprightly Rosette—whose first name is reminiscent of an old French metaphor for an open anus—actively courts her/him, walking close to her/his side one fine evening in the garden, "so as to make her corsage touch fully upon my sleeve: [...] perfectly I felt its pure, firm shape and its gentle warmth." So recounts Théodaine/Madelore before adding, in a precocious refuting of sexual essentialism, that moved by the

---

48 Adrian Kiemander, "Paris Was Always Burning: (Drag) Queens and Kings in Two Early Plays by Alexandre Dumas *père*," in *Essays in Theatre*, vol. 14, no. 2, 1996, 162.

"caresses of my beautiful lover, hearing her speak to me in her soft cooing, I imagine that I am a man."

What produces masculinity, then, is the experience of a sensation: the pressure of the heavy globes of Rosette's breasts. An internal representation too: to be a man is both a fleeting desire and the invention of fantasy, everything but a destiny, an effect of nature, a sad obligation. Madeleine's androgynous instinct delights queer critics, and remained unequaled until, a few years later, Virginia Woolf arrived with her *Orlando*. In a final scene that brings the confusion of the sexes to a crescendo, Madeleine dresses as a woman again to make love to the very effeminate Albert, an obvious invert whom she will attract in her disguise as a man. Then she leaves him to sleep, running to the next room to cover Rosette's moist body with kisses; under the cover of darkness, she won't need to change her accoutrements. The text chastely falls silent there, but still echoes with the heavy breathing of the two lady lovers. On this endless night, the fact that Rosette did not miss the impossible penetration—the desire of which beckoned her from the very first day—doesn't reduce the realism of the novel. Instead, it gives Rosette a queer body *par excellence,* a sensual body free of the need for coitus. In this century that featured some of the finest historical specimens of official homophobia,[49] the feminization of males and the proud virility of these mademoiselles criss-cross each other and turn inversion into the key of all libido, a delirium of desire, a pleasurable halting on the threshold of the act. Better than any other nineteenth-century work, Benjamin Constant's celebrated Adolphe, Baudelaire's crooked obsessions, and the countless fissures in Balzac's monumental oeuvre show this to be true.

---

49 Here we can point to the forensic manuals of Tissot and Tardieu, the tenacious prejudice of the libertarian Proudhon, or the scornful remarks of the Goncourt brothers in their *Journal*.

Constant the Undecided

Did those heterosexist pedagogues do the right thing by putting *Adolphe* (1816), Benjamin Constant's platonic novel, on college reading lists and thus spend so many hours discussing the romantic malaise? "Traitors" that they are, queer critics have asked the question. If the principals of French colleges really wanted to inculcate clearly defined and clearly fixed sexual roles into the curly heads of their charges, nothing could be more counterproductive to reach that pious goal than Adolphe and his contemporaries' storms of uncertainty: their "need for sensitivity," their detachment from the affairs of the world, their onanistic pallor, their unhealthy timidity so close to impotence, their asserted "difference" (as Ellénore says repeatedly of Adolphe), their thirst for the passive role ("I want to be loved," states Adolphe over and over again—in other words, say the QCs, be the woman, be forced), and even the "intimacy" they demand from their masculine friendships. This canonical *bildungsroman* has become the very example of the queer subtext that casts obscurity over the literal text. "Clearly, he is finally scripting his homosexual Oedipal crisis in terms of the socially required model," James Creech puts it.[50]

In this logic, melancholy is the desire for androgyny, a refusal to choose, and even, more physically, the appeal of the sexual organs one refuses to use appropriately, but for which one has yet to find an alternative use—outside of nocturnally polluting the white family heirloom sheets. It matters little if Adolphe's love is directed toward Ellénore; his love softens him, feminizes him, drives him into self-love before turning him into a posturing,

---

50 James Creech, "Forged in Crisis: Queer Beginnings of Modern Masculinity in a Canonical French Novel," in *Studies in the Novel*, vol. 28, no. 3 (1996), 314.

languorous, asexual Olympia: "Masculinity can be conceived as nothing, in itself, but a strategy for defense against contamination" by the feminine virus, in him and all around him.[51] A spasmodic strategy, the superego's reaction, and obviously a failure, since pleasure is manifestly *elsewhere*. Adolphe's inability to break off with Ellénore, to tear himself away from her contagious tears, though without really wanting to satisfy her, is the final proof of his hetero impotence, and not some banal case of compassion.

87

In the beginning is the father, who in the novel incarnates the repulsive masculine figure, but also the fantasy of repressed homosexual incest. His father is a cold presence who, by prohibiting any filial intimacy, makes his adolescent son deeply long for it. His son's wanderings bring him to despair, and he does have his moments of tenderness, too unpredictable to be just paternal, too brusque as well after so many years of distance to be just platonic—these are the happy extrapolations of the queer critics delighted by the improbable touching between Adolphe and his father. These are all factors—distance from his father and romantic onanism—that make Adolphe "an unsure man," to echo the opinion of his entourage. Queer readers have turned this description on its head. Not only is he a man who can't be trusted, he's someone whom we can't be sure whether he's completely a man or not. Of course, this rather feminine undecided gentleman will end up replacing the Count at Ellénore's side, whom he will finally manage to sexually satisfy, and apparently with flair, though Constant's story is happy to settle for vague allusions to that aspect. But when his admiring friends speak of "following his example," the QCs pop up again jubilantly, since they've spotted a clue about his deviancy. Do they want to do what he did with

---

51 *Ibid.*, 306.

her or with him: deflower sweet Ellénore or the shifty Adolphe?

Like the impotence of Crébillon's fops, Adolphe's indecision is not truly a weakness, such as the heterocentric order of the Paris of his time would have it. It is a new source of strength, the choice *not to,* to put off the fall of desire, to entertain all possibilities, all openings, all orifices that pepper the fine surface of the novel or, more to the point, its superimposed surfaces: the refined appearance of the salons of 1830, the impeccable style of Constant the prose-writer, the hairless, untouched skin of the delicate Adolphe. Queer critics are indiscreet enough to attack the author's background and unearth—despite their distrust of biography—elements that would give credit to the hypothesis of a basic ambiguity in Constant's being, or even an infantile perversion quite distant from the pedagogical virtues that our college textbooks grant him. We don't need to look very far. The first page of *Ma vie,* his political and personal memoirs, gets straight to the point, describing the practices of his first tutor, the jewels of a queer treasure, the sadomasochistic impulses, the tutor's sexual deviancy, the pleasures of dissembling and guilt, the little boy's pleasurable passiveness. The tutor was "a German named Stroelin who showered me with blows, then suffocated me with caresses so I would not complain to my father [...], but the thing was revealed despite me, and he was sent away from the house," a sad fate for a man who "proposed we should make a language among us that would be known by us only." This man was quickly replaced by other more classical skirt-chasers whose immorality was conventionally heterosexual, but who instructed him all the same in the reading of Crébillon at the age of ten.

Later in the story, by means of an addition we can find in the *Cahier rouge,* Constant mentions his "Greek loves in Berne" at the time he was knotting a double bind of friendship with Édouard Gibbon and Johann Rudolf Knecht. Further still, between his first female flirtation and his stormy liaison with Madame de Staël, he describes the infamous Baumier, a man "of lost morals" who tried to "overwhelm" him and nearly succeeded, the author admits, in converting him to "the most abject" of existences. It would be no small task to build a bridge between the two irreconcilable shores of Constant's work, the novelist of love and the theoretician of conservative liberalism, the follower of Lamartine and de Tocqueville. In the same way, it would take a bold position to see the parallel between the pleasurable abdication of all will, such as his tutor and the sodomite Baumier incited him to do, and the abandoning of all initiative to the laws of the market, democratic or mercantile—as if the same "invisible hand" caressed the body of the young adolescent and organized triumphant capitalist society unbeknownst to its members, making it no accident that he was one of its most virulent defenders. But we won't let ourselves be caught going down that road.

Lost Allusions

Have we really read Balzac if we see him only as the tireless portraitist of the great, bourgeois, narrative canvas of the times, overloaded with matrimonial and financial themes and nothing else? The very idea that Balzac is above all the most *comprehensible* author (in both meanings, that is, the transparency of the plots and the exhaustive nature of the project) makes queer critics explode in peals of obscene laughter. Critic D. A. Miller's laconic formula echoes that position and sums up the queer point of view: "This world is not so much totally intelligible as it is totally suspicious."[52] Suspicious, first of all, is the monstrous productivity of the great coffee drinker, the master of assembly-line

---

52 D. A. Miller, *The Novel and the Police* (Berkeley: University of California Press, 1988), 29-30.

novels. The QCs, after generations of Balzac scholarship, urge us
to consider the way his novels end, more elliptical than conclu-
sive, his final sentences allusive and opening out—allusion and
not conclusion—like an expansion of time, an expectation of desire (the best example is no doubt the end of *Sarrasine*: "And the
marchioness was lost in thought"), pointing to pleasure in suspense rather than the need to get it over with. Without returning to his atypical libido, this megalomaniac did display a certain suspect tenderness for impotence, "this noble malady that
strikes only young boys and old men" (*Massimilia Doni*). Gay and
lesbian critics have attacked Balzac as the detestable archetype
of the phallo- and heterocentric French corpus, but queer readers
retort by listing the endless inventory of Balzac's dark corners.
In the general economy of Balzac's novels, there is no rumor, gossip, hiccup, or whisper, no volatile words streaming from mouth
to ear, that isn't brandished by queer critics as a constant homage to the world of nancy-boys and lying femmes, concierges and
voyeurs, all in league against the Law of the written sign and the
truth intact.

But what queer reading really likes to celebrate is the profusion of inverted types, scarcely hidden behind some periphrase,
who haunt the crossways of the overly squared-off *Human Comedy*, illusory Champs-Élysées of classic novel-writing. Louis Lam-
bert said of his dearest friend that they had the habit, "like lovers,"
of thinking in perfect pitch and exchanging their dreams. In *La
maison Nucingen* (1837), the sire Godefroid de Beaudenord, so
appropriately named, has at his service a docile little boy with
a name as unstable as his morals ("Paddy or Joby or Toby"), and
who would have done one of Sade's cruelest barons proud. The
boy is "secretive like a prince," with blond bangs and pink cheeks,
"ten years of age and the finest flowering of perversity." The un-
namable object is undressed by the eyes of the British journal-

ist who, finding him too pretty to be a tiger, prefers to call him "tigress," and praises his vices in a portrait both "poisonous and indecent to the highest degree." The QCs also love to linger over ethereal castrati like La Zambinella in *Sarrasine* (1830), characters with ambiguous physiques and very androgynous duplicity like Foedora and Nucingen, and those whose greed and petty manias show them to be compulsive masturbators in Balzac's great orgy. Here, they refer to Poiret, Michonneau, and all the secondary roles of the same type.[53]

More troubling and much better known is the unclassifiable relation between Rubempré and Vautrin, despite the discretion of the writing, as well as Lucien's female conquests, and the homophobic Puritanism of Paris under Louis-Philippe. Passionate friendship, mutual seduction, corruption of a young skirt-chaser by a much less hesitant elder: the relation can't be reduced to a homo-hetero scheme. At the end of *The Human Comedy*, their relation doesn't need to be made any more explicit. The use of the plural and the ostentatious three-dot ellipsis say it all, when Judge Camisot asks Vautrin about "the causes of his affection for M. Lucien de Rubempré." The character of Vautrin, the first of the great ghosts in *The Human Comedy*, and the only one whose homosexuality is clearly announced, doesn't interest queer critics as much because the label is too flagrant. They see in that label an effect of the standard homosexual behavior that is about to be frozen into doctrine. These critics prefer his twisted formulations, his ironic gaming, his constant mockery of hetero norms. When he meets Eugène de Rastignac in the Pension Vauquer in the novel *Le Père Goriot* (1835), he immediately attacks him with a double-edged compliment, an allusion to his power of attraction

---

53 Gerald Storzer, "The Homosexual Paradigm in Balzac, Gide and Genet," in George Stambolian and Elaine Marks, eds., *Homosexualities and French Literature, op. cit.*, 193-194.

over homos in the form of an ordinary hetero compliment (since he's trying to persuade him to marry the unappetizing demoiselle Taillefer): "You are a handsome young man, delicate, proud as a lion and sweet as a young girl, a fine prey for the devil." Here is a scene rich in double meanings served up by Vautrin, as we often see in Balzac's stories. The homoeroticism is justified by the negative, as if by elimination: "I have dug deep into life, and there is only one true sentiment, and that is friendship between men." The injunctions of the social game are formulated in seducer's terms so obvious that the corrupter laughs at them: "Let us each thrust our blade in! Mine is made of steel and never softens, ha! ha!" Vautrin's supposed project to settle in the Americas and become a tobacco planter in itself sounds, in its form as a parenthesis, like a queer manifesto against procreation and setting down roots: "If I don't have children (which is most likely, since I'm not curious to replant myself with my cuttings) ..." Family anchoring, even if it were queer, hardly attracts him—it evokes the sadness of a potted plant.

The Sapphic obsession so dear to the nineteenth century is not absent from Balzac's great construction, but it is combined with effeminate males, reversible intrigue, and sexual disguise, creating a criss-cross of roles and bodies, a geyser of ambivalence where water-tight sexual status (male, female, hetero, homo) springs leaks on all sides. That's the torrential story of *The Girl with the Golden Eyes* (1833), a novel Balzac wrote in Paris while locked away inside a tiny apartment decorated with cashmere, muslin, and Persian hangings, a place quite similar to the theater of his plot, which moved his friend Sandeau to say, as he gazed in astonishment at the decoration, "It's very feminine, but in a nice way, graciously feminine!" Two characters, strangely similar and symmetrically androgynous, vie for the favors of the beautiful Paquita Valdès. On one hand, there is the dandy de Marsay, a delicate Don Juan with slender feminine wrists who nevertheless possesses "a scepter more powerful than that possessed by modern-day kings," and on the other, the fiery and ravishing Marquise of San Réal (Margarita), both angelic and virile depending on the needs of the moment.

When, blindfolded and led passively by the hand into the boudoir of the two lady lovers to be there disguised as a woman, de Marsay realizes, along with the text of the novel, the fantasy of becoming lesbian that so many authors of the time found so moving. But the competition between the two androgynes heats up as the pages turn, urged on by Balzac's pen, sharper than usual for the occasion, until he seems to give the victory to the official male, the natural organ, and orgasm stemming from coitus, since in the end Paquita chooses the Count de Marsay and rejects the Marquise. But as the Count is thrusting his triumphant sword in, Paquita calls out the Marquise's name, and the loser wins the final victory, bitter though it may be, by killing her beloved as her adversary looks on. In these vengeful rectifications, queer readers see all the ambiguous pleasure of Balzac the demiurge. From title to title, his novelistic labyrinth is full of these blind alleys that shelter his characters who, back to the wall, might just (and sometimes actually do) carry out some inappropriate act, and unveil their passion for the same, or relieve themselves by their own hand before setting out again. In two parallel novels from Balzac's last period, *Le cousin Pons* (1847) and *La cousine Bette* (1846)—two works that seem to be above all suspicion when subjected to a literal reading—queer indiscretion discovers solid proof of a heterophobic mechanism that, according to such readers, makes the whole of Balzac's machinery run. This hypothesis is viable, let us add here, only if we forget the hetero liaisons so poignantly invented by Balzac, ones that can't be reduced to a sexual norm, such as in *La duchesse de Langeais* and *Le lys dans la vallée*.

Odd cousins indeed, this heir and heiress impossible to marry off, these two maniacal singular beings, softened rather than hardened by life, who experience their closest friendships "like a marriage" (Pons with the German Schmucke, and Bette with the beautiful Valérie Marneff), and channeling their unused sexual energy into compulsive activity that nickel-and-dime psychoanalysis would consider rather anal: second-hand junk, collectionitis of all kinds, the vice of gluttony around which, for Pons, "all ecstasies" revolve. The twisted intrigues concerning inheritance occupy most of the cousins' time, and a typical Balzac murder of crows circles around them, obsessed with inheriting and duping the innocent—think of La Cibot, Hulot, Hortense, and Count Wenceslas.

But the parallel between the two novels has its limits. Each of the two heroes has his or her own way of escaping the heterosexist family order of their society. Pons' misfortune was to have been "so disgraced by nature," to "be unable to please," which is for a Frenchman "the cruelest of all blows," especially since ill-intentioned people see him "at first sight" as "a well brought up man hiding some secret vice." His friendship with Schmucke is filled with tiny instances of physical contact, peripheral caresses quite the opposite of the homo embrace, like holding hands "to communicate all their soul to one another." La Cibot often rails against "this pair of dusty bachelors" who will never have heirs, two timorous accomplices, though they didn't exactly "pop up, both of them, like mushrooms on this earth." Queer critics jump on this formulation, less for the handsome metonymy of two penis-friends, even if the swelling forth of the image does not displease them, and more for the queerer allusion to the absence of filiation, to an existence without reason or locatable origin. Pons' liver, as it deteriorates, will turn his repulsive face yellow, while La Cibot tries to send for the notary before it's too late. Here is the portrait of an organic and relational disaster that has queer critics applauding.

When it comes to Bette and "the depth of her passionate friend-ship" with Valérie that elicits no end of racy comments from their entourage, Balzac's text comes much closer to the homoerotic mo-tif, from the physical compliments they give each other to their tender embrace. "The most violent sentiment that we know," we are told in so many words, "is the friendship between one wom-an and another." But by kissing each other on the forehead, and wrapping their arms around each other's waists, inverting vices and virtues (one's vices are the virtues of the other, who has "such a need" for them), by constantly changing the description of their relationship (friendship, espionage, sorority, love, maternity), they create a foggy lack of definition that is, we have seen, more strictly queer than any ordinary lesbian couple. Add to that the flagrant differences between the sweet, tender Valérie and the nervous, volcanic Bette that create a bond of complementarity, a chiasmus of characteristics, much more than the complacency of the similar.

Yet the exclusive friendship that unites these cousins to his or her accomplice of the same sex is not what interests queer critics most about these two novels (that are concerned with much more than these relationships). The critics examine friendship accord-ing to its economic and political value, as a radical alternative to the family unit promoted by the bourgeois capitalist society of the times; here, they echo the argument of critic Michael Lucey in an enlightening article.[54] What the queer doctrine has attacked from day one, and what Balzac's curious cousins were bashing, is

---

54 Michael Lucey, "Balzac's Queer Cousins and their Friends," in Eve Kosofsky Sedgwick, ed., *Novel Gazing: Queer Readings in Fiction* (Durham: Duke University Press, 1997), 167-199. This argument was developed in his subsequent work *The Misfit of the Family: Balzac and the Social Forms of Sexuality* (Durham, Duke University Press, 2003).

this system of power relations, solidly organized, that, without allowing any viable alternative, links the profit motive, the transmission of wealth, with family structure, the need to procreate, and heterosexist sentimentalism (the last being the cherry on the bourgeois gâteau). Bette, who stays single, will not inherit, but will cash in the interest on what should have fallen to her, which is just enough to live on; while Pons, on his deathbed, because of competing solicitations, can bequeath precious little to the good-hearted Schmucke.

Over and above the negotiations of legatees that Balzac loves to describe in detail, the lesson of these outcomes, after so much intrigue to extract property from two single people, is clear for queer critics. Interest (in the financial sense), fractioning, supplements, residuals, bread without the butter, the spittle of wealth—that will be swept away by the dominant wave of transmission through filiation—in hetero-capitalist dogma, that's all these people deserve, these cousins, these failures, these homos, these dirty inverts; while the rest—the mass of money after the crumbs fall from the table—goes to married couples, procreators, producers, the only viable defenders of the great human market. The cruel deaths of Pons and Bette seem like a punishment (Balzac as conformist?) of the queer threat they represented for the system of family economy by refusing to get married, procreate, and bequeath to valid heirs. The 700 combined pages of these two novels, before their anti-heroes expire, are certainly enough for Balzac to suggest, with bitter irony, intrigue, and intricacy, what a society would be in which we could bequeath our wealth to our tender friends of the same sex, rejecting blood, family, appearances, and profitable coitus. What would that produce? A queer society.

Baudelaire as Corolla

If we stick to the two recurrent motifs of queer theory, constant sexual permutation (or radical polysexuality) and perversions of the unaccomplished (against the completion of coitus), Baudelaire could vie for—much more so than the classics of the homo corpus, Gide or Genet, even though, unlike those two, he is hardly at all subject to the deviancies of sodomy—the sought-after title of the queerest writer in French literary history. But other than the fact that in the queer manner, the top-ten hit parade mentality has no place (the offensive leftovers of hetero order, they would say), Baudelaire points out as well as any other writers the limits of that approach. In his own way, he seems to anticipate it, but with stakes that are quite different from those of the QCs. He's too queer to really be queer, if we can put it that way. He slips on new outfits too cleverly, or too furtively, to give any purchase to queer representation (the foppish rhyme-spinner or the artificial lesbian), and his refusal of sexual contact is too stubborn, so that even postponed, unaccomplished, or merely fantasized, we can't really associate him with it. And then, last but not least, his taste for changing sex is based on the exclusion of the masculine, be it the lethargy of impotence or the stubbled drag queen, to the benefit of a multiple, provocative, and skewed femininity, decried as much as it's imitated. It is difficult in these conditions to tease him out of any sort of closet. In Baudelaire's work, much to the dismay of old-style gay critics, we don't even find the *brush* of the male. So we will have to look elsewhere, be both more abstract and more precise, if we wish to submit his work to queer rereading.

Baudelaire passes for the literary inventor of modernity, and in his work, it presupposes the feminization of the male. The decisive experience of the crowd, the city, anonymity, all these things in his logic demand a passive body and a sensorial receptiveness that are more characteristics of the female than attributes of the phallus. From the famous "melting away of the self" to the voyeur-spectator of *Le Spleen de Paris* (1869), in Baudelaire's universe everything converges into a generalized desubjectification that is the synonym of the loss of virility, a loss of self that would be to existence what the dilation of the organs, the spreading of the legs, and the loosening of the perineum would be to sexuality—the tabula rasa of ordinary perceptions, the condition for all pleasure. And if writing itself is described as "sacred prostitution," it is also avoids the resurgence of the constrained Subject who, in the tendrils of glory, has so much trouble reaching pleasure. This is the way, according to queer critics, that Baudelaire's obsession with the inversion of the sexes has to be understood: less a fantasy of becoming a woman, or even a lesbian with a hefty member to which psychoanalysis often reduces such games, and more like pure speed, the continual surprise of ceaseless change, the only way to disseminate the self far beyond the bourgeois subject and its Pavlovian organs. Baudelaire is the expert of such permutations, be they ironic or tragic, playful or desirous. The feminine works outward through radiation, contagion, and exhalation, and places the masculine, overexposed, in a sexual limbo from which writing emerges: "The man who, from the beginning, long bathed in the soft atmosphere of woman, in the smell of her hands, her breast, her lap [...] contracted a delicate epidermis and an accent of distinction, a kind of androgyneity," and "the precocious taste for the feminine world, *mundi muliebris,* for that undulating apparatus, shining and perfumed, that builds great genius." He knows what he is talking about. Forget the tired clichés about misty femininity that scandalize some QCs, or the prohibition against women (in the name of their "absence of a soul") entering through the door of a church; what counts here, far from feminine nature, occurs on the level of effluvia, an electric wave, the same imperceptible change in the air that suddenly, as by some miracle, attracts the hetero to a men's sauna and the housewife to her pious neighbor-lady.

Permutation is everywhere. It runs through the motif of the hermaphrodite—"Antiope's hips joined to a young boy's torso" (in "Les bijoux")—by the sensual delight of infantile regression and the hesitating blur of sexual identities, and this ongoing hide-and-seek of the body and soul, like in a parody of old Descartes. While the "mollusk" body of the "egotist" searches in vain for a soul, the poet adrift in the streets is, in the prose poem "Les Foules," "like one of those wandering souls seeking a body." Permutation permeates the tropes that, scarcely made metaphor, graft a suspect protuberance onto the bodies of the "lesbians" (since that was the original title of *The Flowers of Evil*). The cold eyes of these women "who split like an arrow" the faces they look into change, according to the QCs, the metaphor into a veritable dildo, a fake sexual organ strapped by the word "like" onto the waists of lesbians, better to pierce their partners.[55] Permutations become more complicated when Baudelaire fleshes them out in the triangle of street women and their mediating waltz.

Mystic interceders, how venerated they are, these paid-for bodies of prostitutes through whose work two men meet in a breach of time, and touch each other without ever seeing. Precious depository of the syphilitic germ, still spattered with the cold sperm of the previous client, these street-walkers are places and not objects of exchange. They actively link two successive men who, without their knowing, engage in this contact. Here

---

55 For this analysis as well as others suggested here, see Dominique Fisher, "The Silent Erotic/Rhetoric of Baudelaire's Mirrors," and John Barbaret, "Baudelaire: Homo-érotismes," in Dominique Fisher and Lawrence Schehr, eds., *Articulations of Difference*, *op. cit.*, 34-63.

we find an inversion of ordinary sexual roles (the active man and the multitude of passive prostituted bodies) that delights Baudelaire and the queer critics who come after him. "The figure of the prostitute," John Barbaret concludes, "becomes the localized site of relations between men."[56] The permutation is further refined when Baudelaire dedicates, within the poem itself, a lesbian sonnet to his confrere Sainte-Beuve: "For I am before you like a lover." This is not just a man addressing himself lovingly (and ironically) to his brother, but a fictive lesbian with whom he identifies and who, in the poem, herself plays the man with her accomplice, who is also associated, through the double-sided "you," with the masculine receiver of the sonnet.[57] It's not easy finding our way through all this, and we would be caught in the net of the poet disguised if we didn't concentrate on the moist Sapphism of the rest of the poem:

> And then unhealthy evenings, feverish nights came,
> Which make girls fall in love with their bodies
> And make them contemplate in mirrors—sterile
>   voluptuousness—
> The ripe fruit of their Nubility.

Queer critics urge us not to reduce the lesbian motif in Baudelaire to the masculine fantasy of caresses between women, or even to the primary Sapphic identity of Woman. And they are right. Throughout his work, women are the models for disidentification, practically dehumanization, leaving behind nature for artifice—a model in which the poet and the man must find inspiration.

---

56 *Ibid.*, 55.

57 This is a much more twisted schema than Verlaine's in his "Ballade Sappho," where he compares his way of making love to his woman with the way a woman would be with another woman.

These are less individuals than figures given special functions in Baudelaire's triad—the prostitute, the actress, and the lesbian, and between them there is plenty of crossing over, the opposite of simplistic partitioning, according to the principle of synesthesia. They represent not so much unified bodies, sadly reductive integrities, and more amorphous masses, indefinitely extendable, flesh that will soon absorb the male; endless dilations of organic folds, carnate openings, metaphors of body-receptacles that threaten the established order of binary sexuality. They are "urns of love whose great hearts are full," they are "vases of wormwood we drink with closed eyes," they are "the infinite you carry inside you," they are "the gourd from which I drink the wine of memory." Next to these vaginal corollas, real or fantasized, these abysses within the body, the poet imagines the possibility of opening up a new one, the temptation to "inflict on your astonished flanks a wide hollow wound," and "through these new lips, more glistening and more beautiful, I will deliver my venom, my sister."

And in the end the poet, contaminated by the plethora of holes, openings within, and receptacles of flesh, prefers to neglect his meager protuberance to make room within himself for a cosmic vagina, though he does call it a "heart": "I feel an endless abyss opening wide within my being." This is not a particular organ, but a movement into the self; no longer a sexual function but vertigo when faced with the void, not a simple penetration fantasy but voluptuousness springing from abandonment, physical and instantaneous. We must admit, say queer students of Baudelaire, that we do find traces of the desire to be a woman, but not in the meaning of a sexual other—more like the forgetting of self, a definitive confusion of beings.

Everything could well refer back to a primitive scene ("the nebulous times of early childhood") that Baudelaire describes in "Morale du joujou," an extraordinary intertwining of genders and organs, memories and dreams, the irreversible blurring of origins of our hetero borders—or so say the QCs. One fine day his mother introduced him to "Dame Panckoucke" who was dressed "only in velvet and fur." In other words, since Baudelaire states in his *Fusées* that he confused "the smell of fur with the smell of woman": a walking orifice hidden by a skin-cloth and itself covered in tufted fleece, to use the queer contra-lexicon. The lady in question ushered him into a room full of toys from floor to ceiling, "a fabulous spectacle" that "hung like enchanted stalactites"; toys from which the lady asked him to choose, toys to which children speak and which make "their eyes grow wide," toys more real than humans. In "the lustrous cleanliness [...] of this singular statuary" offered by the magical mediator, Baudelaire the child begins dreaming of the reciprocal touching that the treasure incites the little boys to undertake, himself desiring their contact in the midst of this windfall, then retrospectively, within the text of the memory, dreaming of "all those good little boys who [...] have long played with something other than toys."

No use getting bogged down in some boringly tendentious interpretation. That's not the (only) objective of queer reading that, in any case, would rather pull something deeper out of this strange story, as from the many other images that fill *The Flowers of Evil* (1857). For this kind of reading, the fundamental idea— fundamentally queer—is pan-eroticism. It means desexualizing the organs in order to turn the wider world into an erogenous zone, its crowds into a moving orgy, refusing the insertion of body into body to open oneself more fully to unexpected caresses—like any "light caress, the most innocent of all, a handshake, for example, can have a value increased a hundredfold [...] and lead, perhaps, and very rapidly so, to that swoon that is considered by common mortals as the *summum* of happiness," even if it is due to the effect of hashish. Mediating prostitutes, cosmic vaginas, absorbent corollas, toys that urge on salacious games, and an ordinary handshake that practically brings on an orgasm that the bodiless poet refuses elsewhere in his life: this is what makes Baudelaire the queerest of poets, yet at the same time, the space of what limits this sort of approach to a text, a kind of totalization of sex to the detriment of its parts, an animism of the body at the expense of its organs and their functions. It is the constant search for voluptuousness that, in order to surpass hetero precepts, never reaches the effective, local, truly experienced pleasure of *another* sexuality.

Before the explicit twentieth century breaks out upon our shelves with its literature of secrets revealed—to the point of killing said literature—and the wars and the traitors, shrinks, and deviants who come with it, as the imminent wave of novelistic coming-out is about to hit—the more prudent periphrases of the great nineteenth century, in the eyes of the QCs, have the great advantage of tying together, patiently or violently, the complex issues of the love of self: political, economical, and social issues, issues for writing and desire, issues of knowledge and illusions of knowledge. In the midst of the bourgeois décor, the liberal Benjamin Constant placed a timid, quivering inheritor who dreamed of not participating in his own wealth so that people would finally pay attention to him. Flaubert the obsessive wanted nothing more than to go beyond his own stories—intrigues with chastened rebels and fantasy love affairs—in the composing of a single and final "book about nothing." Balzac the productive did his best to shuffle the deck of the great game of sex and turn the comedy of inheritance into a farce of money not owed. Meanwhile, flying in the face of the trade in goods and the hygiene of the sexes, Baudelaire the chemist distilled a discrete poison, hoping that not only would it change our way of writing, but that it would sterilize copulators, change men into lesbians, and make wildflowers grow on the sweat of factories. As for Rimbaud the explosive, he set aside his inkwell and his lover's poses to trade in contraband weapons in the deserts of Yemen. Queer, the lot of them, no matter what their biographers say.

THE MODERN AND ITS MUDDLE

> The question is not, as for Hamlet, to be or not to be, but to
> belong or not to belong.
> —MARCEL PROUST, *Sodom and Gomorrah*

The twentieth century, whose actual chronological limits still divide historians, opens on a rather erratic spectacle of pallid dandies and asexual victims of suicide, that end-of-century pallor that denotes onanism and sterile pleasure. A dawn of ghosts, and hovering over it the freshly minted image, new but already decadent, of the neatly made-up Des Esseintes of *À Rebours* (Huysmans' *Against Nature* or *Against the Grain*) moving through Paris with his loping, striding steps, following a long-legged young man, hoping to inculcate in him the pleasures of "perfidious friendship," or his own pleasure—that he would love to share—at feeling his "satisfaction" inevitably mixed with a "handsome disarray." A tone has been sounded: friendship is no longer passionate but deliberately vicious, pleasure and pain will no longer be furtively linked according to the dice throw of destiny; they will remain incomplete if separated. One asserts oneself; one steps out of the closet; one joins up with specialized societies; one isn't always at one's ease, of course—perhaps there isn't enough material for one's novels—but a new division has come to light, crueler than what came before, because it is less shadowy. It divides hetero and homo as two scientific categories, two natural truths (the first, of course, to be recommended), two pigeon-holes that psychiatrists and doctors, tutors and moralists work to fill with the "objective" results of their research *in situ*. So how can we treat the twentieth-century literary corpus, as prudish as its allusions may be, the way we did Rabelais and Montaigne, Diderot and Baudelaire, all those authors writing before the modern label of homosexuality was invented? This is a question of method, but a thorny one all the same.

In literature, sexual polysemy will no longer possess the insouciance of past centuries. The ambivalence of hetero experience can't be linked to the innocence it had in the romantic times any more, and homo deviancy will cease to be an incongruous exception casting doubt on "normal" love. The latter will be a figure of a new genre, whose tenants and exegetes will work to tease out its specificity. A counter-literature will emerge from this context, sometimes within the dominant corpus, adding its own cohort of new classics to the great love stories of the times: Colette's *Le pur et l'impur,* Gide's *Corydon*, Violette Leduc's *Thérèse et Isabelle*, René Crevel's prose (and his games with the masculine body in *My Body and I*) that ring like an intruder in the Surrealist hetero-sect, the stories of Jouhandeau and the portraits of Cocteau, the first hundred pages of course of Proust's *Sodom and Gomorrah*, the autobiography of Julien Green, and the Hellenizing cross-dressing of Yourcenar. Then, finally and more recently, a bold new literature pushes forward that has no trouble with labels: writers like Guy Hocquenghem, Yves Navarre, Hervé Guibert, Hélène de Montferrand with *Les amies de Héloïse* and Renaud Camus with his pioneering *Tricks*.

While with their predecessors, the gay critics were often happy to sanctify this alternative corpus and turn it into the program for another type of education, queer theoreticians reacted in two ways when it came to the question of method posed by writers in the twentieth century, the century of demands. The first attitude is based on the method imposed by writers in previous centuries, but a little more open given the new freedoms taken by disinhibited writers. Hetero novels had to be "queered" in order to reveal the always constant homoerotic wellspring, and in so doing, invalidating the irritating dichotomy of two literatures. Malraux's heroes go for Chinese guys and their androgynous bodies (which is what the "temptation" of the West really meant[58]); Mauriac's "notables" would have been better off coupling among themselves instead of imposing rigid provincial morality on their wives; and Pagnol's boys didn't climb up the plane trees just to enjoy the view. Within the hetero corpus, queer critics' favorite target is Sartre's fiction; Serge Doubrovsky has already taught us how to resexualize it. Everything is fair game, starting with his confession to Simone de Beauvoir in their interview in *L'Arc* (no. 61, 1975): "I've always felt there was a sort of woman in me." The nausea that afflicts Roquentin would have its roots in sexual rather than existential indecision, the uncertainty about becoming a woman displayed as much by the pain "at the tip of [his] breasts" (after the testicular ache of the frustrated lover) as by the "so fragile" hardness of his penis, or by the curious litany of "from behind" in the midst of his introspection (existence takes him, or thoughts assail him, "from behind"). *Nausea* (1938) also translates a much more explicit disgust for women, their white smoothness, their newborn smell, their strange resemblance with the pub(l)ic garden in Bouville that "smells like vomit." And when he's not dreading the woman inside him, Roquentin is becoming an immense

---

58 André Malraux, *The Temptation of the West*, Robert Hollander, trans. (Chicago: University of Chicago Press, 1992).

cock, a penis-being. These roots that cause him anxiety, his "virile rooting" and the "reason for living" are described as a kind of subterranean turgescence, and his head takes on the appearance and the horrible sensitivity of a glans, and he foresees his own death when he gazes upon this "lurid purple old man" who "is sucking the end of a pencil."

A perverse reading of *Nausea* lingers lovingly over the character of the autodidact, whom Roquentin meets at the library.[59] His name is first interpreted as "an eye of excrement"—Ogier, or *O(eil)-chier,* why not? Before Ogier gets kicked out of the library for having come on to a college student, Roquentin has a kind of monstrous premonition of the event as he stares at the man's thick finger, like "the male sex organ" but yellowed by tobacco, that brushes the student's white hand as it lies on the surface of the table. The hand itself is as bare as the "indolent nudity of a woman sunning herself after bathing." Sartre, we must admit, is doing the queer critics' work for them, so they have to up the ante. They call Ogier's left-wing altruism "masturbatory humanism," and happily slip through the butter, be it metaphor or real fat, spread by the text of *The Road to Freedom.* Daniel Sereno's elegance is compared to "fresh butter." The Germans enter Paris "like a knife through butter," and any agreement with the enemy is like a dry hump ("no more armistice than butter on your ass"). As for the books by his protégé Jean Genet, in *Saint Genet* Sartre compares them to, according to the QCs, so many "tubes of Vaseline." Nothing less.

But besides de-reading the hetero classics—and that includes buttering Sartre's virginal ass—the other queer method of handling the twentieth century consists, more strategically, in de-

---

59 See George Bauer's scatological analysis: "Sartre's Homo/Textuality: Eating/The Other," in George Stambolian and Elaine Marks, eds., *Homosexualities and French Literature, op. cit.,* 312-329.

veloping an oblique reading of the most famous homo pages. As a result, traditional gay criticism, so happy to have a few standard-bearers on its shelves, loses its monopoly. The QCs propose another way of approaching our great fictional homo heroes, from Charlus to Divine and even Michel Ménalque, other than a reappropriation of identity, reductive and even dangerous. Queer critics don't hesitate to denounce, in Proust's and Gide's work, the biologizing avatars of the discourse of the times regarding a "natural science" of homosexuality. The Proustian allegory involves bees and pollen to describe the tactics used by sodomites, and Gide's zoological comparisons seem to spring from a folkloric bestiary, the complete opposite of the queer project, which is to denaturalize, dequalify, and complexify the homo impulse.

In a broader fashion, as it already was for a number of texts from past centuries, the queer alternative presents itself as a change of focus. It's better, say a number of critics out of concern for distinctions, to turn one's playful projector on the ambiguous cases rather than on the out-and-out fairies, on the light caresses and not just the penetration, on the beginning cross-dressers to the expense of the mustached professionals who haven't scared anyone since the days they promenaded their overstated appearances down the corridors of more than one novel—to the point that Gide, Proust, and even Genet, the grand masters of the official homo corpus, whether they like it or not, have become, on the contrary, in queer logic, the apostles of the undefined, poets of the unaccomplished; less subjects anchored in their time and batterers of posteriors, and more the defenders, for posterity, of a much vaguer desubjectification.

A Brush with Gide

For Gide to remain Gide, it is important for his "gate" to be "strait." In *The Immoralist* (1902), Michel feels his desire for Moktir rising as his tender friendship with Marceline is cooling off. In *The Counterfeiters* (1925), Édouard notes in his journal his irrepressible attraction for Olivier, and fails in his attempt to love Laura. Bisexual vacillation, rather banal and marked here by a certain platonic dualism (the desire for the body of the same sex, passion for the soul of the other sex), is less appealing to queer critics than the indecisive in-between to which such vacillation dooms these characters, as they forever draw out the sweetness of refusing to choose, the pleasure of no longer knowing. Quite the contrary, says critic Wallace Fowlie, of those militant gays obsessed with recognition and who, according to him, use Gide too freely, reducing his work and his message in the process. In Gide's work, there is no homosexuality in the meaning of a preference and its libidinal logic, but only these two crucial forms that constitute his sexual "asceticism" (more like Sparta than Athens): renouncing bourgeois norms rather than opting for a sodomite orgy, and what he calls "availability"—what hetero humanists piously call "tolerance," and what QCs want to transform into a complete abandonment of the body to sensual spontaneity.

In that way, the famous dialogue in *Corydon* (1924) reads like an idealistic ode to the love of the same, but very puritan (not very compatible with pleasure, in any case), and hardly anything to do with the *habeas corpus* of gay rights that some militant readers have seen in it. Queer students of Gide read in his work an appeal to all the forms of dilation of the self rather than a rehabilitation of the inverts. In scenes from his autobiographical works, including the *Journal* (1939) and *If It Die* (1926), that tell the story of his sexual touching with Tunisian teenagers, perhaps we ought to wonder, beyond the acts of pleasure, how less pleasant impressions participate in the equation; the feelings of colonial guilt, for example, or this desire to forget as quickly as possible exactly what is happening in the moment—a desire that itself hesitates between forgetting and self-forgetting. It is worthwhile lingering over these primitive scenes, even if it means abandoning the homo sources of his fiction, to better understand the importance of diffuse caresses and brushing, sidestepping and approach, all of this important to Gide's homoerotic identity troubles. In other words—must we say it again?—this is his intrinsically queer character.

In Gide's writing, everything works to put distance (a distance more voluptuous than respectful) between the boys' games that nevertheless reach their final denouement,[60] as with the very playful Ali, the ephebe of Soussa, the arrow of desire, the trace of the desert. First comes the statement of memory, the initial process of the distancing of the subject: the "I see again" of the opening words gives way to a "one another" of a first embrace, then to a shameful "we" when bodies blend together, and in the end to a strange "one" when fusion becomes more abstract. Then comes the pleasure of the voyeur when he steps back to watch Ali's little seduction dance, as if he were excluding himself from the scene, or when he takes pleasure, several years later (at the end of *If It Die*), in the spectacle of a Parisian friend playing the same scene with a young Arab as he looks on. Add to that the distance of other more perverse mediations, as when Oscar Wilde himself procures for Gide the docile, virginal Mohammed, whom he will enjoy alone at first, then share two years later with his friend Daniel B. In that same scene with Mohammed, we see the extension of pleasure far beyond the act and the person of the boy himself, since once he has "reached ecstasy" five times "at his side," he lingers in a "state of shivering jubilation" even after he has left him, to the point that (and here the text is more than allusive) he needs to

---

60 See Michael Lucey's penetrating analysis in the first chapter of *Gide's Bent* (New York: Oxford University Press, 1994).

relieve the pressure by himself alone in his hotel room. Distance once more, rather more racy this time, via the old-fashioned stylistic device of preterition, by which Gide will all but repeat what he did, though saying that he can no longer speak it: "How can I name my emotions upon holding in my naked arms this perfect little savage body, ardent, lascivious, a land of shadow? ..." The three-dot elipses play an equivalent role, as when Gide chooses to fall silent at the critical point of the story: "Clothes fell away, he threw his jacket from him, and stepped forth naked as a god ..." Distance once again—let's hide behind this dune, better to watch them at work—through the exact words the author uses to describe their posture, a discreet copula of their coupling undertaken rather than actually accomplished:[61] "one near the other, yet not one with the other." Like a game of proper distance, the refusal of face to face contact, of the kiss that may come, the unthinkable insertion, for the more playful pleasure of teasing the adversary, catching the one who is offering himself by taking a step backward, or making him laugh—a sound intrusion in this silent scene—when, "seizing the hand he offered, I caused him to fall upon the ground."

Distance, spatial or stylistic, is also distance in time, the voyeur's game, with deviant seduction becoming tender struggle; even the author's preteritive pauses all work to put off a more direct embrace, until finally it becomes highly improbable, even though, surrounded by great discretion, it does take place. Here we recognize the logic of delay so dear to queer exegetes, which tickles them in the writings of Crébillon, Benjamin Constant, or even Madame de La Fayette. Gide, the watchmaker of misunderstanding, the hedonist of postponement, measures his pleasure

---

61 The same spatial copula occurs regularly in *Corydon* to put desire at a distance, with this strange phrase about an "impulse toward desire."

through these tiny delays. If Ali accelerates their little protocol, Gide, a tantric pleasure-artist, prolongs the lead-up, never to descend again; he prefers to step back and interrupt the ascent: "I was not so naïve not to understand his invitation, yet I did not respond immediately." Some time later, returning to the Tunisian beaches, he rediscovers, even before the memory of Ali's salty taste, the equivalent pleasure of endlessly sunning himself on the sand as he delays the moment he will enter the water: "It is not only bathing that I loved, but the mythological expectation." As for love—that sensation as soft and pressing as the half-erection of adolescent games—its only value is in its misunderstanding and lag: "Love, fearing it will be tarnished upon contact with reality, forever puts off its accomplishment" (*Strait Is the Gate*, 1909). Memory as well—this "unformed" flow that delivers the exotic sporting of young adolescence—is for Gide another source of deferral, more distended, more exquisite still: to "unfinish" the scene that is told, to fill it full of silences; better to enjoy it outside the text, by himself, the onanistic nostalgia of an author setting down his pen, there where orgasm is finally accessible.

Sexuality in Gide is defined by its very delay, its distances, by the uncertain play of caresses. It is linked to the brush of a masturbating hand, mutual or solitary (in movie theaters or train compartments), to the unique experience of the unexpected, and never of course to the paradigm of the family, theatrically hated, nor even on the fine sentiment of love (except, perhaps, with Marc Allégret). The condition of this sexuality is the dissolution of the self—summed up by the key word in all of Gide's subjectivity, "denuding"—caused by the loss of all initiative, the forgetting of the slightest intention, the abandonment to the events of the senses, when faced with the impulse for the meaningless act, or Ali's boyish shoulders: "And while all will disappeared, porous as a beehive, I let sensations distill their secret honey within me ..." The sacrifice of all will constitutes, in Michael Lucey's terms, "a sacrifice of masculine gender" that delivers over the passive body that has lost its virility (despite its fear of that process), desubjectified (despite the egotism of the style), to the primary submission of anal sexuality—even beyond Gide's famous refusal of sodomy: to be taken, because first you have been dissolved.

Perhaps the literary paradox of Gide, and not just the sexual one, can be understood in this odd axiom about fantasy: the harmony of the phrase against the convulsions of the body, classical narration to envelope sobbing and trembling, as if Gide's classicism were the only way of expressing its contrary, the mastery of style being the only way to approach the lack of mastery over himself. In that way, through a pleasurable relaxing of awareness, we can understand the recurring term of "curiosity" that Gide uses once he begins describing his "brushes." Curiosity in the sense of unknowing, of a loss of self, the way in which the masterful Foucault invited us to engage ourselves even before queer thought: "The only kind of curiosity, in any case, that is worth acting upon with a degree of obstinacy: not the curiosity that seeks to assimilate what it is proper for one to know, but that which enables one to get free of oneself." The rest of Foucault's text taken from *The Use of Pleasure* can be applied as much to Gide's sexuality as to the work of queer critics in general: "After all, what would be the value of the passion for knowledge if it resulted only in a certain amount of knowledgeableness and not, in one way or another and to the extent possible, in the knower's straying afield of himself?" [62] Sometimes the QCs themselves lose track of things, lose their way, and lose us in the process.

114

---

62 Michel Foucault, *The Use of Pleasure (The History of Sexuality, Volume 2)* (New York: Vintage, 1990), 8-9.

Proust Inside Herself

Similar to the critical apparatus in the last edition in the Pléiade collection—longer than the novel itself—*In Search of Lost Time* (1913–27), from its very first English translation, set off a veritable deluge of secondary texts, from pastiche to essay to hagiography, among which his queer commentators, for once in their careers, were actually in the minority. And blackening white sheets of paper is no sin against ecology for them! Here, all queer theses have been stated, the last being the fundamental Sapphism of the narrator of *Lost Time.* According to critic Kaja Silverman, his love for Albertine is an "explicit lesbian love," while Elizabeth Ladenson proposes a rereading of the entire novel informed by the author's "lesbianism."[63] In more recent years, Proust has become the backbone of the queer corpus, the bible of gay dogma. To the QCs, he is to Foucault what a year of internship is to a year of teaching: the indispensable praxis and the enlightening creation of a work, during which we learn (and take pleasure in) so much more than from books. These two names, Proust and Foucault, illuminate the queer firmament. Proust's canonic opening sequence from *Sodom and Gomorrah* called "La race des tantes" ("The Race of Fairies") sits on the same shelf as Foucault's great conversations about "friendship," And *Sodom and Gomorrah* is the only French text quoted as often as Foucault's *The History of Sexuality* by queer pedagogues. The "sentimentality" of Proust's homoeroticism plays a founding role for the homo-reading of any literary work, alongside Foucault's sexual constructivism, as Leo Bersani reminds us. Dedicating a meager sub-section of this book to Proust is something of an insult to the passion that thousands

---

63 See Elizabeth Ladenson, *Proust's Lesbianism* (Ithaca, NY: Cornell University Press, 1999).

of homo-readers feel for him. With all respect to the fervent, that's not a reason not to be brief. Once again, we will turn to what is least flagrant, and to do this, we will travel through the successive layers of the queer reading of Proust, which is particularly heavy with sediment.

The first layer, the first paradox, the most classically queer: the choice of the most banal scenes, childhood rituals or hetero fumblings, at the expense of those passages—too often commented—dedicated to homosexuality. From the very beginning of *Swann's Way*, the portrait of Legrandin emerging from the church at Combray is a gold mine:

> He made a profound bow, with a subsidiary backward
> movement which brought his spine sharply up into a
> position behind its starting-point [...]. This rapid recovery
> caused a sort of tense muscular wave to ripple over
> Legrandin's hips, which I had not supposed to be so fleshy;
> I cannot say why, but this undulation of pure matter,
> this wholly carnal fluency, with not the least hint in it of
> spiritual significance, this wave lashed to a fury by the
> wind of an assiduity, and obsequiousness of the basest sort,
> awoke my mind suddenly to the possibility of a Legrandin
> altogether different from the one whom we knew.

Let's compare a queer commentary from Gregory Woods to the interpretation of this excerpt by a conventional critic (Jack Murray) who sees this portrait as the simple presentation of a snob. A snob, perhaps, but one who "takes it up the arse" and whose generous buttocks are "the obverse of the cruising queen's ceaselessly roving and winking eyes: their role is to attract penises and then to receive them. Such buttocks are no more passive than a

brilliant society hostess who attracts men into her salon."[64] If
we follow Gregory Woods, the great Baron of Charlus here is
overshadowed by the plump Legrandin, a simple uncertainty
in the land of fairies, yet who manages to organize high-society
receptions between his protective buttocks, in the shelter of his
rectum-salon.

The second stage of reading, less meticulous, more general:
the function of the Proustian comedy of manners as a circulat-
ing movement of gossip, the transmission of scandal, and the continuous postponement (like desire in Gide's case) of a truth that is
more or less accessible. *In Search* extends the principle of effluvia
to the confines of the possible; diffuse words and desires, always
repeated by other mouths, first started by Saint-Simon's *Mémoires*
and Madame de Sévigné's letters, then greatly refined by Balzac.
Aunt Léonie, who is above all suspicion but desperate at having
no spectacle to watch from her window during the afternoon *si-
este*, ends up spreading rumors about the dogs dozing in the sun.
This proves by its very absurdity, according to queer critics, that
nothing in Proust's world escapes the gossip principle. Here we
begin to reach the third layer of reading, inspired this time by the
Deleuze-tinged remarks of Monique Wittig about Proust's "war
machine." The gay motif of *In Search* is not sprinkled like splashes
of color or rose cameos, an impressionistic logic based on identity, but proceeds by contagion, insinuated first by inoffensive
opening descriptions (like those of Legrandin), then radiating
outward to take in the entirety of the text, the totality of the plot,
and "making of the 'real' world a completely homo world."

Homosexuality in Proust's work is not a fact, an event, but a
way of broadcasting, gradual and invasive. Here we meet up with

---

64 Gregory Woods, "High Culture and High Camp: The Case of Marcel Proust,"
   in David Bergman, ed., *Camp Grounds: Style and Homosexuality* (Boston:
   University of Massachusetts Press, 1993), 129-130.

Roland Barthes' thesis of the "pandemic of inversion" in Proust, and Leo Bersani's view of a gay subjectivity that, from hearsay to disguise, lives "according to the exuberant model of continuous expansion," and the conclusion of Gregory Woods that all high-society life quickly takes on the appearance of a "carnival of queens." Then there is Jean-Paul Aron's fine idea that, by comparing Jupien in front of Charlus to a "flower woman" who "thrusts out his backside" with the coquetry of an orchid (a necessary meta-flora for all gay reading), Proust was not suggesting that homosexuals are floral, but rather that flowers themselves belong to the phylum of fairies. As Gilles Deleuze wrote in *Proust and Signs*, "Homosexuality is the truth of love." This expansion of homoeroticism beyond small desiring subjects, beyond the homo and hetero labels, onto plants, lost words, and even drafts, all the way to a blur of complete undefinition, makes Proust the great chorus master of the entire queer doctrine:

> And here was this word "so" applied to Morel with an extension of meaning of which Charlus was unaware [...]. So that the people who were "so" were not merely those that he had supposed to be "so," but a whole and vast section of the inhabitants of the planet, consisting of women as well as of men, loving not merely men but women also, and the Baron [...] felt himself tormented by an anxiety of the mind as well as of the heart, born of this twofold mystery which combined an extension of the field of his jealousy with a sudden inadequacy of a definition.

Infected with this contagion, language works back upon itself, irony is possible everywhere, error becomes truth. Before we find out more about it, doesn't the innocent Françoise warn us, because she believes that Charlus as well as Jupien would make

"a woman very happy," that, yes, on that point, "the Baron and Jupien are the same sort of person"? Based on this third layer of
reading, the layer of homo-contagion, we find the joyful lucubra-
tions of Proust's style: his descriptive spirals, his endless sentences, his sumptuous logorrhea, his "sheer quantity of speech"
that "stands at the opposite end of a stylistic spectrum to the
costive taciturnity of Ernest Hemingway, which so loudly prof-
fers as its principal meaning 'virility.'"[65] There is an effeminate
quality to Proust's sentences, a hypersensitivity in his generosity
with epithets, and even, through his use of style, the only trans-
parent confession about the narrator's true orientation. Does he
not tell us about Charlus in *The Prisoner*—after more than 3,000
pages of text—that it "is almost impossible for men of his sort to
hold their tongues"? Any chatty person would be caught with his
pants down.

Here is the perfect introduction to the fourth and final floor of
Proust's house, such as queer reading has remodeled it, with that
typical mix of innovative design and kitschy taste: the erasing of
normal limits between men and women, thanks to the development of the theme of inversion, finally forming the crucial Proustian figure, the most androgynous of all: the "man-woman." The
twisted polysemy of this expression also designates, throughout
In Search, a dated explanation of male homosexuality as an almost scientific reference to the theme of the hermaphrodite (the
Zwischenstufen, or "third sex" of Viennese theories of the period)
and even, much more broadly, the intrinsic androgyny of the
true creative personality that exhibits its art in Proust's work in
no finer a manner than by drifting between these two "halves."
For the QCs, everything in Proust's novels helps destabilize the
fragile border between masculine and feminine. This includes

---

65 *Ibid.,* 132.

the narrator's not very credible affirmation of his heterosexuality, which is invalidated by his position as a voyeur looking on at homosexual sport (in the Montjouvain bushes in the case of Vinteuil's daughter with her girlfriend, and through a keyhole—or is that a glory hole?—to see Charlus being flagellated at Jupien's). Such is Albertine Simonet's determined attitude, she who, beyond her Sapphic emotions, should have been called Albert.

This is the barely imaginary portrait of these men "in their households" (Jupien or Saint-Loup), or the famous paradox that, boasting of "the strength of his virility," Charlus makes the narrator think of a woman. On all sides, we see the incredible mix-and-match of sexual identities at the source of every desire: Rachel's flirtation with a dancer who reminds her of a woman, Saint-Loup's fantasy inspired by a woman playing the role of a man, or the words of the lesbian actress Léa according to whom Morel has "the same taste as women for women themselves." To top it all off, there is this curious sexualization of the narrator as a woman when he describes his more abstract relationship to knowledge, in a sentence so open-ended it would defuse almost all its perverse readings: "[...] dangerously, I allowed the funereal pathway of Knowledge, destined to be painful, to widen its way through me." But as always, when a queer critic caresses a text against its grain, as unready as it might be, the most original discoveries await us in the tiny recesses of its body, the headiest pleasures in unsuspected enclaves, unattractive to the official libido. After the handsome architecture of Proust's dwelling, it is only right to present at least one example of what queer Proustologists can unearth therein, peeking into a pantry, nosing into a corner of the boudoir, or, if the case calls for it, near these "relief stations," less proper, but where relief and release go hand in hand.

From the dwelling to its moldings; from architecture to micrology: let's set aside the recurring question of whether *In Search* is a giant body erogenous in all its parts, or a vast pavilion shot through with glory holes. Whatever the metaphor is, queer reading becomes more acute in the forgotten corners and casually discarded accessories—for example, in the tea service. Among the overhangs of meaning and folds of details that QCs explore with a lubricious eye (a body as corpulent as the real Marcel was reedlike), no doubt the best example has to do with the codes relating to tea, as illustrated by a stimulating article by the young critic Jarrod Hayes.[66] To hell with suspense, let's just deliver the rather silly, but seriously troubling thesis at issue here: "The possibility that taking tea is a code for homosex infects not just the most sacred of Proustian passages (the description of the madeleine) but the entire system of Proustian memory; thus, the paradise gained from taking tea might, in fact, be Sodom."[67] A triple entwining code, quite far from the transparency of the ordinary signifier, backs up this thesis: at the turn of the century, the expression *prendre le thé* (to take tea) secretly designated homosexual copulation, and the accessories involved (the teapot, cup, tea-ball) referred to the figurative meaning of public urinals, those hidden places where, to protect their reputations, lovers of the same sex would meet at nightfall for furtive, fleeting pleasure. There is no lack of sources from the times that give credit to these codes. The dictionary put together by Jean-Paul Colin and Jean-Pierre Mével dates the first homo connotation of "teapot" back to 1890, and associates "cups" with public washrooms as early as 1925. There are allusions in painting to tea rituals (like the Ondine-style lesbian scene painted in 1928 by Jules Pascin entitled *L'Heure du thé*), and the overheated memoirs of authors as objective as the hetero

---

66 Jarrod Hayes, "Proust in the Tearoom," in *PMLA Journal*, vol. 110, no. 5, 1995, 992-1005.

67 *Ibid.*, 993.

Brassaï.[68] We could add, just for show, the premonitory and sub-
tly pictorial comparison of the not very queer Toulouse-Lautrec:
"When I get a hard-on, I look like a teapot."

The code, in any case, is an open secret. Using a typically
Proustian double displacement (a hetero mistaken meaning
and a more queer dyslexia around the French word *pissotière*,
meaning both "fountain" and "urinal"), the narrator's own *maî-
tre d'hôtel* is astonished that Charlus spends so much time in the
public conveniences: "Certainly monsieur le Baron de Charlus
must have caught a disease to stay so long in the pissery. That's
what it means to be an old skirt-chaser." Hidden as an error in
grammar, Françoise commits a similar slip on the same word:
"She never said *pissotières*, but—with a slight concession to the
custom—*pissetières*." As for the other segment of the triple
code—the one involving the sodomite connotations of tea—the
narrator makes no bones about it, conjuring up the triplet autho-
rized by this ritual of polite society: "The two aspects ['vices' and
'will'] had to be equally considered when monsieur de Charlus
went every day with Morel to take tea at Jupien's house." Charlus
himself provides the final link, if that can be said of a triangular
code, by mocking, at the Verdurins' house, the urinary "ugliness"
of these old "frozen coffee cups": "Whatever else, do not put them
in the salon, for we may forget ourselves and believe that we have
entered the wrong room, for they look exactly like chamber pots!"

Here again, the queer motif of *In Search* is found less in the
simple use of a homo code of the times and more in the disguising,
dispersion, and deviation of that code, both by people involved
or innocent bystanders. Little by little, tea steeps its double and
triple meanings throughout the text. Its acrid vapors issue from
the least suspect of passages, inciting queer critics to take one

---

68 Jarrod Hayes, *op. cit.*, 1000.

step further (a step too many, perhaps?) by attacking—pleasure in blasphemy, the sweet violence of interpretation—the sacrosanct scenes of Proust's cup of tea. What if we reread the page of the madeleine, that so many schoolboys were forced to decipher, as the description of a homosexual act? A first surface reading would slip between the folds of the voluptuousness of the text:

> No sooner had the warm liquid [...] touched my palate than a
> shudder ran through my whole body. An exquisite pleasure
> had invaded my senses [...] the effect which love has of
> filling me with a precious essence [...]. Whence could it have
> come to me, this all-powerful joy?

This passage is too well known, too precious to the Republic of Letters, to miss a chance to push our advantage a little further and turn it around, sully it, strip it of its pious robes of "the pleasure of memory" to which generations of teachers have limited it. We know that the narrator, in this scene, was dipping his biscuit according to the well known expression, and that the biscuit in question was the vulva-shaped madeleine. All the QCs had to do—and it was easy—was mingle two apparently incompatible French readings (the first by Serge Doubrovsky, the second by Philippe Lejeune) and then conclude, very queerly so, that Marcel Proust, in his solitary pleasure, was imitating the lesbian caress of two vulvas, a contortion demanding a certain agility from its participants, and from the author, a twisted sort of sentence, in its posture and its deviance, that suddenly reveals to the perplexed reader that "memory and therefore writing are linked to masturbation, urination, and defecation"[69]; as is, as secret and as disturbing, the relation of the invert to his "troubling truth."

---

69 Jarrod Hayes, *op. cit.,* 1000.

But since the image of lesbian masturbation leads us away from sodomite pleasure, we need only join this scene to another, more ambivalent still, of the narrator playing with Gilberte under the boughs of the Champs-Élysées (where his explicit "discharge" remains ambiguous, sperm or feces according to the reading) to discover, at the end of this winding, onanistic, and mimetic path, the clear denouement of true anal pleasure. This orgasm scene on the Champs-Élysées is not placed by chance between the ritual (that follows it) of tea in the family, and the narrator's visit (preceding it) to the public urinals on the avenue, where a "cool smell of enclosure fills [him] with a pleasure not at all of the same kind as others [...] but on the contrary a consistent pleasure against which I could steady myself, delicious, peaceful," and creates within him a sensation "that offered me, not enjoyment of the pleasure it procured me in excess only, but descent into the reality it did not unveil for me."

It's easy to understand that, in such a state, the slightest hetero embrace disguised as child's play, as on the bench with Gilberte, is enough to make the narrator immediately explode in the childish relief of a more adult desire, the hetero fallback of a homo pleasure tasted only moments before—a pleasure inspired more by "tea" than the intruding madeleine. Some will criticize the queer exegetes and their coded readings, and justifiably so, for betraying their promise, which is to leave open the echoing polysemy, and instead installing, as seen here, similar to the unique and prudish meaning preached by hetero readings, a table of equivalencies in itself rather rigid. And so we would get something like this: tea = sodomy; madeleine = lesbian fantasy; urinals = homo desire; Gilberte = dildo. But if they managed in their commentaries to preserve the unequaled ductility of Proust's texts, they would be the competition, not the critics of his writing. And we would know as much.

Genet De-penetrated

More than any of our authors, Jean Genet has been the object of a prodigious transatlantic transference. His best biographers and finest exegetes have been American, most often coming from traditional gay studies, or gay fiction itself, as in the case of writer Edmund White. This doesn't make the job any easier for their successors. The challenge Genet presents for queer reading is, above all, a sexual overload that is not very compatible, at first sight in any case, with the QC gaming with themes like the writing of disturbance, the blurring of roles, allusions to the in-between, and even an inversion that will not dare admit itself. From *Funeral Rites* to *Querelle of Brest,* from *The Miracle of the Rose* to *Our Lady of Flowers*, the mythic profusion of fairies and queens, cruise artists with raucous voices and knights of the round hole, the epiphany of a style that shows these creatures coupling, Alcibiades-style, licking then tearing each other apart: all this seems to invalidate the logic of ellipses and the connotative suggestions so dear to queer critics. This is a paradox from an author who, from his dark wanderings to his self-assertions, incarnates the accomplishment of every queer precept, starting with his hard-edged marginality. But, once more (one last time), the queer approach is able to deflate the sexual audacity of Genet's least forgettable pages and turn them, often following their true intent, toward his favorite motifs: gender confusion, the desubjectification of bodies, and the opacity of desires proven more by unaccomplished caresses than virile penetration.

Queer critics insist that when it comes to Genet, orgy is only an ostentatious illusion that a certain logic (hetero or, at least, identity-based) of a sexual "give me more" wants to pass off as an overblown portrait of homo "truth," while silencing what in Genet's novels insinuates itself between the bodies in their pleasure:

uncertainty, pain, mystical sentimentalism, and, always, inaccessible fantasy. As an illustration of these queer counter-readings, let's look at (in the original text, not yet expurgated, published by Les Éditions de l'Arbalète) Genet's 1943 masterpiece, the emergence of an ex-prisoner from the Fresnes jail onto the orderly French literary scene at mid-century. Here we are talking about *Our Lady of the Flowers.*

The first angle of attack starts with a trivial, negative remark that opposes the assertive power of the characters who are all "that way" (Divine, Darling, Mimosa, Our Lady, and Gorgui): there is very little anal sex in *Flowers*. Homosexual sexuality, whose omnipresence in this work has no precedent in French letters, is mainly non-penetrative in nature, more oral than anal, more tactile than rectal. The reading of one single (and explosive) sex scene reveals the recurrence of verbs of play, rather than verbs of sex (fighting, embracing, falling) or seduction (seeing, smiling), and the use of the third person plural turns individual initiative into something indistinct. On the other hand, fellatio undergoes a double displacement, first toward a metaphor of penetration via the mouth, which is rather curious in this context, then toward a renunciation of the story, pure and simple. Both displacements are illustrated by this surprising bit of preteritive lip service censored in the 1951 Éditions Gallimard publication:

> How hard it is for me not to mate the two of them better, not
> to arrange it so that Darling with a thrust of the hips, rock
> of unconsciousness and innocence, enters deeply, desperate
> for happiness, with his heavy smooth prick, as polished and
> warm as a lovely column in the sun, into the waiting mouth
> of the adolescent murderer who is pulverized with gratitude,
> brimming with sperm, thinking, 'Oh, Darling, everything
> because it's you.' That could have been, but won't be.

For the narrator locked away in his cell, fellatio could stand for sodomy, but it will not take place, except between two refusals in the text, the time it takes to declare the impossibility of it all. Another remarkable counter-performance: the frequency in Genet's work of soft-ons, half-erections, sudden and fatal detumescence. These events have various explanations depending on the case, but their relation to the distancing of fantasy (a distance always maintained) won't let us reduce them to some psychological or physiological cause. There is Paulo's panicked, shrinking dick when he imagines fucking with Hitler (in *Funeral Rites*). Blood drains from the member outside of the sex act when the fervor of love and the emotional trance remove the eroticism from bodies so detached they have stopped belonging to themselves (Divine speaking of Archangel: "She doesn't even have a hard-on"). Once more the soft-on strikes when the games of permutation and disguise destroy all will, leaving the floor open to the more random waltz of destiny (as in the three-character scenes: Divine, Darling, Our Lady, or Divine, Darling, Gorgui). The final debacle, and an odd denouement, provides the key moment of the final trial, when Our Lady will try in vain to justify "her" crime to the jury. A soft-on is the only valid motive this sixteen-year-old street kid facing the guillotine can find for his act, and he says so in his clear, laconic voice: "The old guy was fucked. He couldn't even get it up." On a queer note, we could add that the old guy had no more use in this world because he couldn't get it *down* any more either.

To avoided sodomy and lethargic organs, we should add—to discourage the sexual simplicity of the first readers of *Our Lady*—the constant confusion of gender, above and beyond the parade of drag queens that Genet serves up, beyond the apparent division of the characters (between active and passive, fairies and pimps), beyond the whirlwind of *he's* and *she's*, and *he's* becoming *she's*. We have seen that kind of thing before, of course, in medieval epics and court coquetry, romantic friendships and Proust's androgynes. But here, gender confusion sometimes turns into the inexplicable. That's the case with the name of the character who gives us the book's title, though nothing in the novel explains it. Why does the young Adrien Baillon—the most masculine of Montmartre homos, virile between the sheets and a risk-taker on the streets, an active sodomite and hardened criminal, the curse of fairies everywhere and Darling's brother-in-arms—answer to the queenly nickname of "Our Lady of the Flowers"? What might he have done outside the pages of the book to deserve the name? The question haunts queer critics. A single crucial scene, a rare penetration, could have feminized Our Lady, but as a result of a pretty queer sleight of hand, everything goes back to normal. Divine prepares to sodomize Our Lady, a provocative challenge, when the feeling of the teenager's stiff member against her belly suddenly throws her into this "state of delirium that she knew only too well," and, left once again to the strength of the male, makes her grab Our Lady's sex with both hands and guide it av- idly toward her anus. In another scene, Our Lady's attempt to dress up in drag fails in curious fashion, revealing the complexity of role-playing in Genet's universe. Hesitating at first, Our Lady ends up slipping on the dress offered by Divine, but once they reach the cabaret, an erection blossoms underneath and deforms its lines. In an act of solidarity, the giant Seck helps hide that em- barrassment by wrapping himself around the teenager, making sure the evidence enters the space between his powerful thighs. This firm constraint calms him so much that Divine will have to pep him up again with a brief bout of fellatio. But Divine ends up deeply disappointed. Excited by this little game, she wants to take big Seck into her, but he turns his back on her, preferring to hellenize Our Lady.

Here is the queer analysis of this tortuous game of back and

forth: as soon as a fantasy blooms in Divine, the kind that might
be based on a more stable sexual role (dress up Our Lady as a
woman, try and sodomize him, or be Seck's passive lover), the
uncertainties behind the exchange of bodies put off its realization, slowly blurring its edges and turning it into an undefined
"objectless fantasy" without a direct relation with the scene at
hand. Like Our Lady's cock between Seck's thighs, the fantasy is
imprisoned in the unexpected turn of events, which distances the
protagonists from it, and the mechanical reflexes of bodies. The
fantasy adjusts to the first condition by emptying itself out of all
content, so that the passing situation will not invalidate it, then
adapts to the overly physical spontaneity of the organs in question by turning itself into a reflex, an image without a referent,
pleasure without mediation: "Of its own volition, the murderer's
hand fumbled for his hard cock [...]; finally, he jerked off until he
came, shot his wad in the old man's choking, toothless mouth."
Neither guilty obsession nor necrophilic cliché, this fantasy, according to the QCs, is the ordinary reflex of an adolescent hand,
far from the sophisticated imaginary structures used by psychoanalysts and normative critics to reduce its mystery and lock it
up in a prison of their device.[70]

Sexuality in Genet's work proceeds from a basic indetermination. When it's not involved in the evaporation of its object,
fantasy—as in these formulations—can't be distinguished from
a vague reflex of the body. Sex roles themselves are pure vola-
tility, asserted by the gaudy makeup smeared by an accidental
embrace, proclaimed by a theatrical name when nothing else in

---

70 The exception, perhaps, are the remarks made by the psychoanalysts Jean
    Laplanche and Jean-Bertrand Pontalis about fantasy, themselves quoted
    by the QCs to shore up their reading of Genet. Fantasy is not "the object
    of desire" but the "framework" of its creation. It is a stage on which "the
    subject exists as a desubjectivized form."

the character calls for it. The terms of address themselves keep hesitating. Nicknames are chosen from an endless repertory, alternating the formal and the familiar within the same dialogue. And emotions, these organs of the soul, entangle contrary expressions to the point that we soon forget the water-tight psychology of old novels about love. Such is the case when the village kids try to lapidate Divine, still a child, and in the midst of his/her rage, he/she feels an uncontrollable love for them. Or when Genet's passion for Jean D. inspires "enchantment" for his miserable corpse. And again, from *Querelle of Brest* (1947) to *The Thief's Journal* (1949), to the extent that Genet's ascetic love has become one with the crimes and cowardly betrayal he commits, in spite of himself, at the expense of the very ones who have filled him with wonder.

So there is general confusion between fantasies, genders, roles, names, and emotions; confusion between the characters who all want to become "beings of imaginary choice" to the point of taking on "the troubling appearance of being multiple," itself a confusion of sexual organs that Genet compares in his writing to various objects (as when Querelle associates the jewels of thievery with his testicles). A cosmic confusion that underpins his celebrated loving transcendence, the purity of filth in the midst of the worst turpitude to which so many lyrical flights in Genet's work aspire. Confusion as well—and here is the primary issue for queer theory—that casts us back to the fundamental experience of desubjectification, as Genet himself experiences when, sitting in a train facing an older passenger, he suddenly feels his entire being enter that of the old man (in a magical episode that obsesses his biographers). This is less an act of "communication," a word dirtied by power, less a "becoming-the-other" stained with Christian humanism, and more a sudden breaking down of all barriers between beings and things, perception and "reality," a new limitless porosity, the least human source of pleasure and the least existential source of anxiety that can be.

Just as dimly felt disturbances haunt every character—disturbances of disguise, origins, lost names, of the body abandoned by the two partners—this loss of self troubles Genet's prose more radically than the instances of sexual fury, compulsive fellatio, and tender sodomy celebrated by the writer's first gay readers. After centuries of a literary history marked with the seal of an all-powerful but scarcely bodily subject (or a founding subject whose body could not be transformed, no more than a necessary envelope in the Christian tradition), the theme in Genet's writing of getting free of the self will validate the queer motif of desubjectification through the experience of the body, and by that very act give sexuality—in the broadest sense of the term—a truly ontological dimension that was missing, according to the leaders of queer reading, among the libertines of the Enlightenment and the inverts of Albion. In that way, to get free of oneself became, with Genet, the alpha and omega of the written body. But here, instead of adding up his writing games, to which the QCs have dedicated endless obscure pages of literary theory (resubjectification through the pen, sexual inversion through style, etc.), we prefer to quote, from the depths of the speaking body, Genet's sweetest illustration of ontological desubjectification, which also constitutes its most intimate limit: that of love of self before representation, setting his work apart more clearly within twentieth-century literature and its elegant aporias. Here I refer to the case, taken from *Our Lady of the Flowers,* of the salutary effluvia of the prisoner's fart, such as described by the author:

> I have already spoken of my fondness for odors, the strong
> odors of the earth, of latrines, of the loins of Arabs and,
> above all, the odor of my farts, which is not the odor of my

shit, a loathsome odor, so much so that here again I bury
myself under my covers and gather in my cupped hand my
crushed farts which I carry to my nose. They open to me
the hidden treasure of happiness. I inhale, I suck in. I feel
them, almost solid, going down through my nostrils. But
only the odor of my own farts delights me, and those of the
handsomest boy repel me.

132

The unbearable smell of someone else's fart indicates the end of
the dialectic, the inanity of old hetero altruism. But in order not
to remain with the negativity of a single stink, with the trouble-
some odor of someone else, Genet invites us under his covers,
where no one else can approach the absent center, or dirty the
clean being. And there, the smell of his own fart reveals to the
body, suddenly and more fundamentally, a nameless pleasure,
pure of all discourse, a pleasure far from the Other made possible
only by the perfumed disappearance of the Subject, here underneath the prison blankets. This passage is perhaps only anecdotal, if such a category can exist in Genet's work (or, more impor-
tantly, in prison), a confession provocative by its very sincerity,
but that points to the unshareable sentiment of the self, the tiny
distance from oneself that only the narrator—in solitary shame
and windy pleasure—can reveal to himself. Desubjectivized
through the circulation of desires, through the ceaseless slippage of sexual roles, what the subject savors with the intimate
experience of the fart, far from a sexual impulse, is the smell, in
a way, of his own absence. And since Genet could queer even his
own flatulence, and summon up all his power of forgetting from a
single olfactory memory, nothing in the body can now be spoken
of as it normally was for so long, in the corpuses of glory and their
flowery frontiers, in the closeted order of fine oppositions.

SO AS NOT TO FINISH

Sexual relations never stop not being written.
—JACQUES LACAN, *Seminar XX*

In the hollows of the text as in the games of sex, if there's one thing that queer thinking abhors, it's the idea of *finishing*: arriving at the end, exhausting desire, immobilizing the meaning of a work, getting off then going to sleep, proud of a job well done and the questions answered. What the queer thinking refuses to let us say about it, in self-defense, it itself is tempted by, if only to offer as fodder to its readers a bit of coherence, and the texture of a discourse that can be transmitted—that's what *finishing* means. It began by concluding (and we meekly followed it on this point) that all the rapprochements of sex and text were possible, necessary even: the pleasure of bodies and the disturbances of reading, metaphors and word play, parallels and peccadilloes. We can only agree with it when it comes to texts that, even in French, even the most classical, open like corollas, swell like organs under the eye of pleasure, a reader's who is in no hurry to finish. The disturbances of sexual identity and the subtexts of the love of self do in fact stir all great literary works, which themselves could only have been born from an initial deferral: that which separates the project from the writing, the plot from the signifier, and that between these poles—sometimes far apart—opens the split into which all systematic pleasures of continuous suspicion can insinuate themselves. Such is the queer text.

But what can we say about the inverse proposition that queer thinking risks forgetting about bodies altogether in the name of its insistence on the text, its textualism; in the way it sees sex as a text, the ordinary body as a corpus, the real (urgent) homoeroticism of two skins coming together like the desires awoken in a reader, sitting in his armchair, for the ambiguous heroes of a novel? What about the panicked attraction when faced with a real glory hole compared to the more controlled need to sully the authors we most cherish? It is difficult to follow queer critics on that side of perverse reading. And not to see therein, besides the comfortable transference of coolly desexualized university types, an avatar of the strictly intellectual excesses that have divided university campuses over the last thirty years: the referent of reality against the text-as-everything, hermeneutic reasoning against the suspect signifier, the humanists of meaning against the subversives of doubt. And has this last group, by lodging sex at the heart of the text, by verbally billeting it there, not naïvely adopted, with little critical distance, Jacques Derrida's famous 1967 formulation that triggered so many vocations: "there is nothing outside the text" (il n'y a pas de hors-texte)?

The light that queer critics shed—at least, some of its tenants, more careful and less jargonizing—on our pious heritage is now accepted. That an invert may be sleeping the sleep of the polluter behind so many of the great hetero figures of the French novel—that's what awakens somnolent texts, and loosens the vice of our usual reading. Instead of the doctrine of the literary Subject, a compact character or omnipotent author, we may well prefer the trembling of desubjectification, the ecstasy of the self diluted, its dilation, its scattering—this is what gives textual analysis a little more critical intelligence and pleasure in its reading. And that it might be more interesting to drift and shift between two sexes, to hesitate over one's orientation, to experience the sensations that belong to each of the "roles," whether we are readers of flesh or heroes of a novel: only limited minds and bodies could contest that idea. Long before the QCs, a good number of free (or tormented) spirits thought that way too. Poor Daniel Paul Schreber who, between two attacks, said it himself on Freud's couch and in his diaries: "It would be closer to the realization of desire, *in the life hereafter,* were we finally delivered of the differences between the sexes." Yes, the ideal of the *hereafter,* the way queer readers speak of the Literary Text. In other words, let us pay tribute to queer free spirits, their playful reading and their inquiring vigilance, and let us make sure that the joyous discoveries made before them by a handful of prophetic neurotics do not fall into forgetfulness.

But there's a but. It has to do with the textualism we just mentioned. And also, what we said at the very beginning: the complacency of an esthetic based on a single blurring, a single oscillation, a reversible concept, a discourse that tends, by its very reading, to desexualize a novel's characters under the pretext of finding the weak point. By replacing bodies with metaphors and desires with ambivalence, real life loses its erotic sting—if we may use that expression "real life"—by preferring the interstices of disturbance and intransitive hesitation to the firmer platforms of pleasure. The famous business about "homosexuality" that queer thinkers have criticized since Foucault, calling it a reductive category, does turn out to have something in common with some of their statements. Let's listen to Foucault, if we might, who, speaking of Prussian psychiatrists in the 1870s, seemed to be anticipating his own disciples on university campuses: "Homosexuality was constituted the day when it was characterized [...] less by a type of sexual relation than a certain quality of sexual sensibility, a certain way of inverting the masculine and feminine in oneself, [...] when it was removed from the practice of sodomy and cast as a sort of internal androgyny."[71] This passage, in itself an old one, from an explicit story to a circumventing discourse, from a crudely anatomical designation to a more artistic (here, with scientific pretentions) blurring of internal ambiguities, will no doubt bring to mind a similar evolution in America a century later. This was the queer method against gay "essentialism" in the name of a more subtle form of "truth." Queer vigilantes say they detest this kind of "truth," but sometimes, with their chatty nuances, they tend to rebuild on its ruins.

If we wanted to be perfidious, we could even add, two pages further on in the same Foucault book, a description that recalls the pleasure, so typically academic, of a new power over texts and their meanings, and gives a more sociological explanation of the queer vogue through one of these "pleasure-power spirals" that flower so easily in the domain of *discourses* about sexuality: "These polymorphous conducts were actually extracted from people's bodies and their pleasures; or rather, they were solidified in them; they were drawn out, revealed, isolated, intensified, incorporated, by multifarious power devices."[72] This is the only limit—but it may be insurmountable—to the queer approach, even when applied to the French corpus: it is simply one more *discourse* about sexuality, as performative as it may believe it is (but who ever shot his wad while reading Balzac?), and not a real practice; frightening sometimes, but of greater interest to the poet-artisans and novelist-architects who dropped one day,

---

71 Michel Foucault, *The Will to Knowledge*, Robert Hurley, trans. (London: Penguin, 1998), 43.

72 *Ibid.*, 48.

long after their deaths, into the freshly washed hands of a few American academics. Criticism is still negative; exegesis is still production; the questioning of arguments is still a dodge from the body, or its embalming in a book-sarcophagus. The glory hole of the queer critics was just another fine image, and not a real way through.

INDEX

FRANÇOIS CUSSET is the former director of the New York-based French Publishers' Agency, and is currently professor of American Studies at the University of Paris, and a series editor and contributor to many journals on both sides of the Atlantic. He is the author of *French Theory* (University of Minnesota Press), a pioneering account of four decades of intellectual and political life in the United States.

DAVID HOMEL, born and raised in Chicago, is a Governor General Literary Award-winning translator and writer who lives in Montreal. His most recent books include the translation of *The Last Genet: A Writer in Revolt* by Hadrien Laroche (Arsenal Pulp) and the novel *Midway* (Cormorant).